JAN 19 1990

Electronic Fund Transfer Systems Fraud

Electronic Fund Transfer Systems Fraud

PALADIN PRESS
BOULDER, COLORADO

Electronic Fund Transfer Systems Fraud

ISBN 0-87364-490-5
Printed in the United States of America

Published by Paladin Press, a division of
Paladin Enterprises, Inc., P.O. Box 1307,
Boulder, Colorado 80306, USA.
(303) 443-7250

Direct inquiries and/or orders to the above address.

PREFACE

The need to assess potential levels of fraud in electronic fund transfer (EFT) systems has been apparent for some time. This report presents findings of the first pilot effort to develop such estimates on the basis of data obtained directly from a sample of banks.

It should be recognized that obtaining fraud data directly from banks represents a major breakthrough. Banks have traditionally been reluctant to share any information that might shake the consumer's confidence in the banking system. Similarly, bank record systems have not been organized to permit easy identification of EFT-related loss incidents. Despite these difficulties, a selected sample of banks agreed to participate and to provide data for this study. Total anonymity was assured to all participants.

Particular thanks should be expressed to the Association of Reserve City Bankers for their enthusiasm and cooperation, and to 16 of their member banks who actively participated in this effort by being a part of the Study Panel. It is our hope that the data from this survey will benefit the financial community, policymakers, and the general public.

Steven R. Schlesinger
Director
Bureau of Justice Statistics

EXECUTIVE SUMMARY

During the past decade, the Nation's banking and payment system has become increasingly dependent on rapidly evolving computer-based technologies, collectively known as electronic fund transfer (EFT) systems. There are three groups of EFT technologies: those which support retail banking, including the automated teller machine (ATM), point-of-sale (POS) terminal, and home banking; those which support corporate banking, including wire transfer, automated clearing house (ACH), and cash management; and those which support internal bank functions, including on-line teller terminals and computerized check processing. Although these technologies have been a boon to financial institutions and consumers, they also provide an electronic environment that is potentially fertile for criminal abuse. Given the phenomenal growth in the use of EFT and the resulting potential for EFT crime or fraud, it is necessary to develop knowledge about its characteristics and estimates of its incidence. Yet while crime concerns in EFT systems have been heightened by the phenomenal growth in the use of such computer-based systems, there are no valid data on EFT fraud. To date, the available information has been limited to newspaper accounts of celebrated incidents or analysis of questionnaire surveys with low returns.

In response to this lack of data, the Bureau of Justice Statistics (BJS) funded this study to collect consistent, incident-level data directly from a group or panel of banks; such data could then be used to assess both the nature and the extent of EFT fraud. In addition to being a first effort at collecting consistent fraud data from banks, the study sheds light on computer crime in general.

While the scope of this study encompasses all EFT technologies, the focus is on the ATM and wire transfer technologies; being the oldest and most widely used of the EFT technologies in their respective retail and corporate banking areas, they do serve as appropriate bell-weathers for their respective areas. The transaction volume sustained by each of these two technologies is not only significant but growing. Another reason for focusing on ATM and wire transfer is the feeling among industry experts that there are thus far few fraud-related incidents occurring in the other EFT technologies, including ACH (which together with ATM and wire transfer can be considered to be the mature EFT technologies). This does not, however, imply that it has been easy to obtain fraud-related information in the ATM and wire transfer areas. Indeed, a host of problems --including multiple data repositories, definitional differences, procedural differences, and reluctance to share certain pieces of information -- have plagued the data collection effort. Nevertheless, in collaboration with the Association of Reserve City Bankers (ARCB), a Study Panel of 16 ARCB member banks was constituted. Analysis of the data obtained from the Panel banks has yielded several interesting and policy relevant findings.

First, in regard to ATM fraud, the key findings are:

- In 1983, it is estimated that there were 2.7 billion ATM transactions (i.e., withdrawals or deposits) involving $262 billion. Activity increased in 1984 to 3.0 billion transactions, resulting in a dollar volume of $291 billion.

- Because of the requirement of Federal Regulation E (Reg E), detailed fraud-related information is available at banks for those ATM incidents involving an accountholder complaint. Less complete records are maintained on incidents involving only bank complaints.

- The Panel banks supplied 2,707 1983 and 1,480 1984 ATM incidents, 42 percent of which were determined to be potentially fraudulent, involving, as examples, unauthorized use of lost or stolen cards, overdrafts, and "bad" deposits.

- In most respects, the 1984 ATM incidents are comparable to those for 1983; any differences cannot be interpreted as a trend but can most likely be accounted for by the year-to-year variation in the underlying statistic.

- Lost or stolen cards are the leading cause of ATM fraud and bank losses. Present in many of these incidents is accountholder negligence, which, partially because of Reg E requirements, is contributing to bank losses.

- Banks could reduce ATM fraud by effectively utilizing computer technology when designing their ATM systems.

- Bank losses per incident are small (roughly $200 per incident), but scam-related incidents in the study sample underscore the potential for large single-incident losses (in the thousands of dollars).

- Based on both the 1983 and 1984 data sets, the annual nationwide bank loss due to ATM fraud is estimated at between $70 and $100 million. On a per transaction and dollar volume basis, ATM fraud losses are at this time significantly lower than credit card fraud losses.

Second, in regard to wire transfer fraud, the key findings are:

- In 1984, roughly $668 billion per day was transfered over the FedWire and CHIPS networks alone, representing a 48 percent increase since 1980.

- Data collection in the wire transfer area has been more difficult than in the ATM area, primarily because wire transfer frauds are rare and there is no formal mechanism -- like Reg E -- for requiring their documentation. As a result, the extent of wire transfer fraud could not be estimated, as summary data on wire transfer fraud and loss could not be readily obtained.

- A total of 207 wire transfer incidents occurring in the past six years were obtained from the Panel banks. Not surprisingly, the vast majority of the incidents are errors leading to either fraudulent absconding with funds or exposure without loss of principal, as opposed to intentional fraudulent acts.

- As in the ATM area, computers could be used more effectively to prevent wire transfer fraud, especially those resulting from clerical errors.

- The exposure (i.e., potential loss) per wire transfer incident averaged $942,450. However, if one considers only those incidents occurring within the past three years, the average exposure is $1.6 million.

- Wire transfer managers are projecting a significant increase in their annual fraud losses in the next five years, thus supporting the observation that there exists a high level of fear of fraud in the wire transfer community.

- According to wire transfer managers who have experienced wire transfer frauds, the current fear of fraud is greater than warranted. Indeed, the banking industry should be as concerned about ATM fraud as it seems to be about wire transfer fraud.

Third, in regard to the panel approach itself, it can be stated that valid and consistent fraud-related data can be obtained directly from financial institutions. The willingness of the banking community to participate in this effort and the enthusiasm generated by the resultant findings are evidenced by the following events:

- An unexpectedly high percentage of the invited banks chose to participate in the study. While 18 banks were initially invited to participate, it was hoped that 12 would accept. In the end, 16 banks accepted an invitation to participate.

- The Study Panel banks have provided over 4,000 ATM incidents (which occurred in 1983 and 1984) and over 200 wire transfer incidents (which occurred between 1980 and 1984), as well as important summary data on ATM fraud and loss.

- Nearly half of the respondents to an attitudinal survey of wire transfer managers have indicated their willingness to participate in future fraud-related data collection efforts.

- The two study-related Special Reports published by the Bureau of Justice Statistics (BJS) have received coast-to-coast radio, newspaper, and television coverage.

- The banking community has expressed great interest in this study, as evidenced by several well-received presentations of the study at conferences sponsored by the Bank Administration Institute (BAI) and the American Bankers Association (ABA).

Although this study has provided insight into the nature and extent of EFT fraud and has demonstrated the viability of the panel approach, it should still be regarded as a pilot effort and its findings should be considered preliminary. Obviously, a 16-bank panel cannot be representative of the more than 14,000 commercial banks in the U.S. Moreover, the Panel banks are all ARCB-member banks, each with assets of over $1 billion. Thus, for the future, a larger and representative panel of banks should be established to provide an on-going source of information on EFT fraud. Such an effort could make use of the same data collection instruments as those employed in this pilot effort, inasmuch as the instruments have been developed to (i) facilitate data collection, coding and analysis; (ii) be straightforwardly adopted in an operational environment (so that they could be used by the banks for administrative and investigative purposes); and (iii) be easily implemented on a computer (as has been done in regard to the pilot effort's analysis).

Finally, the remainder of this Executive Summary provides a framework in which to consider the above cited study findings. The study background and approach are summarized below.

Study Background

In order to systematically examine the nature and extent of
EFT fraud, it is essential that a common understanding of the
underlying technologies be established. Yet identifying EFT
fraud is dependent on first recognizing the types of activities
that constitute "electronic fund transfers". EFT systems are a
type of payment system, meaning that EFT systems facilitate the
exchange of value or money from one party to another. Since
there are at least three other major payment systems (i.e.,
currency, checks, and credit cards) in use today, it is important
to recognize the distinguishing feature of EFT payment systems:
although currency, checks, and credit card payment systems are
primarily paper-based, EFT systems are primarily electronic-
based. Indeed, EFT systems are defined as payment systems in
which the exchange of value, or information necessary to effect
an exchange, is represented or facilitated by electronic
messages.

While the above definition is useful, inasmuch as one must
define EFT before defining EFT fraud, EFT systems are perhaps
more often defined in terms of the specific technologies commonly
identified with EFT. As indicated earlier, of the retail
technologies, only ATMs are widespread at this time; POS and home
banking are still in their planning and pilot testing phases. It
is estimated that in 1983, the nationwide useage of ATMs
accounted for 2.7 billion transactions (i.e., withdrawals and
deposits), totalling $262 billion. The corresponding estimates
for 1984 are 3.0 billion transactions, totalling $291 billion.
The most pervasive corporate EFT technology, however, is wire
transfer. In fact, wire transfers constitute the dominant form
of non-cash transactions in the Nation, as $668 billion was
transferred per day over the CHIPS and FedWire networks in 1984.
This dollar figure represents a 48.4 percent increase over that
of 1980. Put another way, given a gross national product in 1984
of roughly $3.7 trillion, one might say that during the course of
the year the GNP moved through the wire transfer system 47 times
or once every 1.1 weeks!

As EFT technologies proliferate, so does the potential for
fraud. In regard to potential vulnerabilities in their ATM
operations, bankers are especially sensitive about the growing
fraud experiences of the credit card companies, especially in the
area of card counterfeiting. Federal Regulation E (Reg E) has
also increased the bankers' concern over ATM fraud, as it limits
cardholder liability, even when the cardholder is negligent. In
the corporate banking area, the concerns are even greater, as
enormous sums of money are transferred each day through the
various wire transfer networks.

With this heightened concern, it is interesting that no
commonly accepted definition of the term "EFT fraud" has emerged
in the literature. Nonetheless, the ability to differentiate
frauds that can be attributed to the presence or operation of an

EFT system from others that occur in financial institutions is a prerequisite for analyzing the nature and extent of EFT fraud. Ideally, a definition of EFT fraud should act like a sieve -- catching and identifying certain activities as EFT fraud while letting others slip through. At the same time, it is important that the definition be sufficiently broad so that the impact of EFT technology on the incidence of fraud can be fully assessed. In this report, EFT fraud is defined as follows: EFT fraud is any crime, whether or not prosecuted under special computer/EFT laws or traditional law, that would not have occurred <u>but for</u> the presence of an EFT system.

In spite of both the phenomenal growth in the use of EFT systems and the increased concern for EFT-related fraud, there are no valid data on EFT fraud, as pointed out earlier. There are several reasons for this, including:

   (i)   the proprietary nature of EFT systems and the corresponding concern over potential competitive disadvantages that might result from the release of operational data;

  (ii)   the wide variations in definitions, procedures, and categories used by financial institutions to record transactions, fraud events, and charge-offs for sustained losses;

 (iii)   the technical and practical difficulties in identifying the occurrence of an EFT fraud, either while in progress or after the event;

  (iv)   the uncertainty about the legal status of specified actions that may (or may not) constitute a crime in a given jurisdiction;

   (v)   the common practice of handling EFT violations by in-house security or personnel procedures rather than by the standard criminal justice system;

  (vi)   the absence of a comprehensive or central data source -- like the FBI <u>Uniform Crime Reports</u> -- for capturing EFT data;

 (vii)   the nonexistence of a standardized and comparative data base against which EFT losses can be measured on a trend-line basis; and

(viii)   the relatively recent development of EFT technologies, some of which are still in their initial implementation phases.

Nevertheless, despite the above cited difficulties, several attempts at collecting EFT fraud data have been made. Four attempts deserve mention -- they include a file of computer abuse cases compiled at SRI International by Donn Parker and Susan Nycum; reports filed by financial institutions with their federal regulators; files on federal bank crimes kept by the Federal Bureau of Investigation (FBI); and a study on financial fraud conducted by the American Institute of Certified Public Accountants (AICPA). Unfortunately, none of the available data sources on EFT fraud can provide valid data for measuring the nature and extent of EFT fraud. Each has only limited information, and all have problems from a statistical perspective. Further, although several offer a possible source of information, the potential exists only if major changes can be made in the collection processes --changes which seem highly unlikely to occur. These sources offer perceptions or clues about the nature of EFT fraud, but do not provide an adequate data base for statistical analysis.

Study Approach

In light of the above stated shortcomings of the earlier efforts at obtaining EFT fraud data, it was obvious that valid and consistent data could only be provided by the banks themselves. To this end, the study proposed to obtain EFT-related data directly from a small panel of commercial banks. The study was able to convene -- with the help of the Association of Reserve City Bankers (ARCB) --a panel of 16 banks. This panel approach has several advantages. First, it provides a "clean" source of data that could be used confidently to draw conclusions about the nature and extent of EFT fraud. Second, it allows for the acquisition of a consistent set of data so that such relative measures as the ratio of EFT fraud losses to total EFT transactions can be determined and then employed to estimate nationwide losses due to EFT fraud. Third, it sensitizes the banking industry not only to the actual EFT fraud problem but also to the need to develop valid and consistent measures of the problem. Fourth, if the Panel was to be enlarged and surveyed on an on-going basis, it would provide a continuing barometer of EFT fraud.

For both the ATM and wire transfer areas, three types of data were obtained from the Panel banks: (i) incident-level data (in order to assess the nature of ATM and wire transfer fraud), (ii) summary-level data (in order to assess the extent of ATM and wire transfer fraud); and (iii) background data (in order to understand and explain the resultant findings). In addition, a nationwide survey of wire transfer managers was conducted --in particular, their attitudes concerning fraud were assessed. For each type of data, a special data collection instrument was developed; the instruments were provided to the Panel banks and arrangements were made to obtain the requested data in as expeditious a manner as possible. The obtained data was subsequently coded and entered into a computer for subsequent analysis. The 1983 and 1984 ATM data were at first analyzed separately and then together, while the 1980-1984 wire transfer data were combined and analyzed as one, merged data set.

Finally, obtaining fraud data directly from banks represents a major breakthrough. For many obvious reasons, banks are reluctant to share any information that might shake the consumer's confidence in the banking system. On the other hand, casting the few headline-capturing EFT fraud incidents in perspective and in relation to the total transaction volume is perhaps one reason 16 ARCB member banks -- out of a total of 18 invited banks --agreed to participate in this study on an anonymous basis. Another reason is the knowledge provided by the study concerning EFT fraud, at both the individual bank level and the aggregate level. While data from a sample or panel of banks could provide a valid and on-going measure of the nationwide EFT fraud problem (in much the same manner that A.C. Nielsen Co. rates television programs based on data collected from a national panel of some 1,200 households), it is obvious that a 16-bank panel is inadequate for such a purpose -- as mentioned earlier, it could not be representative of the more than 14,000 commercial banks. Again, it should be stated that the study documented herein represents a pilot effort and its findings should be considered preliminary.

ACKNOWLEDGMENTS

The authors would like to acknowledge the support of the Bureau of Justice Statisitcs (BJS). In particular, we would like to recognize the contributions of Ms. Carol G. Kaplan, who as the BJS Grant Monitor, provided critical feedback, suggestions, and encouragement throughout the study.

The study could not have been carried out without the interest and cooperation of the Association of Reserve City Bankers (ARCB). Special thanks go to Mr. Anthony Cluff, the Executive Director of the ARCB, and to the 16 ARCB member banks which accepted our invitation to participate in this pilot effort and to be a part of our Study Panel. Although we cannot identify them by name, we would like to acknowledge the many Panel bank personnel who spent countless hours responding to our data requests and reviewing our findings.

A number of other individuals have made essential contributions to the study. Dr. Kent W. Colton acted as a key study advisor; Mr. George L. Fosque and Ms. Sherry T. Davis made extensive contributions in the early stages of the study; Mr. James A. McClure developed and coded the sophisticated data entry and analysis system; and Ms. Jo Ann Bohmfalk, Mr. David Godinho, Ms. Phyllis deFano, Ms. Judi Bloomingdale, Ms. Gerda Van Thielen, and Ms. Debra Northrup provided skillful typing and editing of the various study reports.

TABLE OF CONTENTS

Page

LIST OF EXHIBITS

1 INTRODUCTION

During the past decade, the Nation's banking and payment system has become increasingly dependent on rapidly evolving computer-based technologies, collectively known as electronic fund transfer (EFT) systems. As summarized in Exhibit 1.1 and discussed in Section 1.1, there are three groups of EFT technologies: those which support retail banking, including the automated teller machine (ATM), point-of-sale (POS) terminal, and home banking; those which support corporate banking, including wire transfer, automated clearing house (ACH), and cash management; and those which support internal bank functions, including on-line teller terminals and computerized check processing. Although these technologies have been a boon to financial institutions and consumers, they also provide an electronic environment that is potentially fertile for criminal abuse. Given the phenomenal growth in the use of EFT and the resulting potential for EFT crime or fraud, it is necessary to develop knowledge about its characteristics and estimates of its incidence. Yet while crime concerns in EFT systems have been heightened by the phenomenal growth in the use of such computer based systems, there are no valid data on EFT fraud. To date, the available information has been limited to newspaper accounts of celebrated incidents or analysis of questionnaire surveys with low returns [Colton et al., 1982]. In sum, as recognized by the Association of Reserve City Bankers (ARCB) [1983], "there is a lack of empirical data on the nature and extent of crime in electronic payment systems."

In response to this lack of data, the Bureau of Justice Statistics (BJS) funded this study to collect consistent, incident-level data directly from a group or panel of banks; such data could then be used to assess both the nature and the extent of EFT fraud. In addition to being a first effort at collecting consistent fraud data from banks, the study sheds light on computer crime in general, which, as noted in a recent study by the American Bar Association (ABA) [1984], "is a problem of substantial, and growing, significance."

While the scope of this study encompasses all EFT technologies, the focus is on the ATM and wire transfer technologies; being the oldest and most widely used of the EFT technologies in their respective retail and corporate banking areas, they do serve as appropriate bell-weathers for their respective areas. The transaction volume sustained by each of these two technologies is not only significant but growing [Tien et al., 1984]. Another reason for focusing on ATM and wire transfer is the feeling among industry experts that there are thus far few fraud-related incidents occurring in the other EFT technologies, including ACH (which together with ATM and wire transfer can be considered to be the mature EFT technologies). This does not, however, imply that it has been easy to obtain fraud-related information in the ATM and wire transfer areas. Indeed, as indicated at appropriate points in this report, a host of problems -- including multiple data

repositories, definitional differences, procedural differences, and reluctance to share certain pieces of information — plagued the data collection effort. Nevertheless, the banks which agreed to participate in our Study Panel and their association --the ARCB -- have been quite cooperative; their support and interest have not only made this study possible but also made it a significant and important effort.

The remainder of this section addresses important background information regarding EFT systems and EFT fraud. Section 1.1 defines EFT and describes the various EFT technologies, in particular the ATM and wire transfer technologies which constitute the focus of this study. Section 1.2 provides a definition of EFT fraud and duscusses the fraud related vulnerabilities of ATM and wire transfer systems. Section 1.3 describes past efforts to collect data on EFT fraud. Finally, Section 1.4 outlines the scope of the report.

1.1 EFT TECHNOLOGIES

In order to systematically examine the nature and extent of EFT fraud, it is essential that a common understanding of the underlying technologies be established. Yet identifying EFT fraud is dependent on first recognizing the types of activities that constitute "electronic fund transfers". Accordingly, this section begins with a definition of EFT, followed by a discussion of the principal EFT technologies in use today.

EFT Definition

EFT systems are a type of payment system, meaning that EFT systems facilitate the exchange of value or money from one party to another. Since there are at least three other major payment systems (i.e., currency, checks, and credit cards) in use today, it is important to recognize the distinguishing features of EFT payment systems. To illustrate these payment systems and to highlight their differences, we consider how they might impact the purchase of a home video recorder from a store.

Financial transactions using currency are relatively simple. In our example, the customer hands the clerk the appropriate amount of currency and takes the recorder. This paper-based transaction involves little direct support from financial institutions.

Payment by check increases the complexity of the transaction. In this case, the customer writes a check for the appropriate amount and takes the recorder. To transfer the check's value into a more negotiable and useful form, the store owner deposits the check at the store's financial institution, whereby the store's account is credited. While this is, again, a paper-based transaction, notice that check transactions are intimately tied to financial institutions, which provide a support structure for transferring the checks and maintaining the account balances.

Purchasing the recorder by credit card is an even more complex process because both

1

Exhibit 1.1

EFT: Primary Categories and Technologies

Category	Technology	Description
Retail	Automated Teller Machine (ATM)	Remote terminal linked to a financial institution's account records. ATM users (i.e., accountholders) may carry out several simple financial transactions, including deposits, cash withdrawals, account transfers, balance inquiries, mortgage and loan payments, and other bill payments.
	Point-of-Sale (POS)	Remote terminal which links a retail establishment to one or more financial institutions. The POS terminal may verify check payments, authorize credit purchases, or transfer funds from a customer's account to a merchant's account (for payment of purchase).
	Home Banking	Service which permits accountholders to access their account records and to initiate financial transactions at home (through a computer terminal). Home banking users (i.e., accountholders) may access account information (balance, transaction history, cancelled checks, etc.), make payments, or transfer funds between accounts. Initial versions of this system include the use of a touch-tone telephone for bill paying purposes.
Corporate	Wire Transfer	Service which allows large dollar transfers -- between and among financial institutions, the Federal Reserve, and corporate customers -- to be made through a digital communications network.
	Automated Clearing House (ACH)	Service which takes magnetic tape based transaction information from originating financial institutions, sorts it, and then transmits it to receiving institutions. ACH is primarily used for direct deposit of payroll and government checks.
	Cash Management	Service which allows corporate customers to electronically access their accounts. In addition to receiving account balances and history, customers may transfer funds between accounts and initiate wire transfers.
Internal	On-line Teller Terminal, Computerized Check, Processing, etc.	Systems which allow financial institutions to electronically process their transactions.

purchase and loan functions are involved. The customer hands the clerk a credit card so that the clerk can prepare a credit card invoice. The customer signs the invoice, takes a copy of the invoice and leaves the store with the recorder. At month's end, the customer receives a bill from the credit card company and would typically pay the bill by check. Again, the transaction (i.e., the invoice) is paper-based; further, because credit cards are typically tied to checking accounts, credit cards require the support structure provided by financial institutions.

Electronic fund transfer include a wide range of payment technologies and systems, more than one of which could be used in the purchase of the recorder. For example, the customer could use an ATM to get currency from his/her account to pay for the recorder; or he/she could have the clerk use an electronic check guarantee system -- part of a POS system -- to assure that his/her check would be honored; or he/she could hand the clerk a debit card to insert into a POS terminal through which the customer's checking account and the merchant's bank account are instantaneously debited and credited, respectively. The institutions involved in the EFT support system are, for the most part, the same as those involved in the check support system. However, the primary difference is that the EFT transaction is carried out by electronic signals. Thus, while the check support system is primarily paper-based, the EFT support system is electronic-based. In sum, EFT systems are payment systems in which the exchange of value, or information necessary to effect an exchange, is represented or facilitated by electronic messages.

While the above definition is useful, inasmuch as we must define EFT before defining EFT fraud, EFT systems are perhaps more often defined in terms of the specific technologies commonly identified with EFT. In this regard, each of the EFT categories and technologies identified in Exhibit 1.1 is discussed below.

Retail EFT Technologies

The three primary retail EFT technologies -- ATMs, POS systems, and home banking -- provide a wide variety of consumer-oriented EFT banking services that facilitate both the transfer of information (e.g., check verification and balance inquiry) and the transfer of funds (e.g., cash withdrawal and bill payment). Of the three technologies, only ATMs are widespread at this time; POS and home banking are still in their planning and pilot testing phases. Yet based on recent growth patterns, POS and home banking systems could become widely used in the near future. Interestingly, as further discussed in Section 5.3, the growth of ATM networks have fueled the growth of POS systems. It is fitting, therefore, that in the retail aspect of this EFT fraud study, we should focus on ATMs.

Automated Teller Machine (ATM)

ATMs are remote terminals linked to a financial institution's account records that allow users to perform various financial transactions including cash withdrawals, deposits, account transfers, balance

inquiries, mortgage and loan payments, and other bill payments. Access to ATMs is regulated by the use of magnetically-encoded plastic cards (i.e., ATM cards) and a personal identification number (PIN), that, depending on the financial institution's policies, may be numeric or alphanumeric, range from four to eight digits, and be either customer-selected or bank-assigned. ATMs may be either "free standing" or "through-the-wall". Free standing ATMs are placed away from the bank's physical facility, in such locations as shopping centers, office complexes, airports, and busy street corners. Through-the-wall ATMs are physically located on the grounds of the financial institution. Many ATMs, such as those on street corners or in bank vestibules, are accessible 24 hours a day.

Exhibit 1.2 depicts the principal components of an ATM system. These include the ATM, the ATM switch, the bank's computer (which maintains accountholder records such as account balances), communications lines, the network switch (if the system has network capabilities), and the computers of other banks. To see how these components function in tandem, consider the steps necessary to allow an accountholder to withdraw $200 from an ATM operated by the accountholder's bank. When the user inserts his/her card into the ATM, a device "reads" the data encoded on the card's magnetic strip. The ATM switch "behind" the ATM recognizes that the card belongs to an accountholder of the bank that operates the ATM and will therefore route information between the ATM and the bank's computer. (In the presence of a local or proprietary ATM network, there is no need for such a switch; a direct communication line automatically routes information between the ATM and the bank's computer.) The ATM then "asks" the computer if the card is valid (e.g., Has the card been reported stolen? Has it expired?). Upon verification, the ATM instructs the user to input the PIN. Again, the ATM asks the computer if the user has input the correct PIN. Once the correct PIN is input (the cardholder is typically allowed three to six attempts to enter the correct PIN), the ATM presents the user with a menu, by which the user indicates what type of transaction is desired (in this example, a $200 cash withdrawal). The ATM then asks the computer if the accountholder is allowed to make this transaction (e.g., Is the account balance greater than $200?). If the computer authorizes the withdrawal, the transaction is performed: the $200 is dispensed; the user's account is debited $200; the transaction is recorded on a transaction log; a transaction receipt is printed for the user; and, if the ATM is camera-equipped, a photograph is taken of the user.

With the introduction of regional and national ATM networks, cardholders are no longer limited to using ATMs owned by the financial institution at which they have an account. Rather, cardholders may perform transactions on any ATM owned by a financial institution that is a member of the same network to which the cardholder's financial institution belongs. Suppose the user in Exhibit 1.2 wishes to withdraw $200 from an ATM not operated by his/her financial institution. When the user inserts his/her card, the ATM switch recognizes that the card

Exhibit 1.2

ATM: System Description

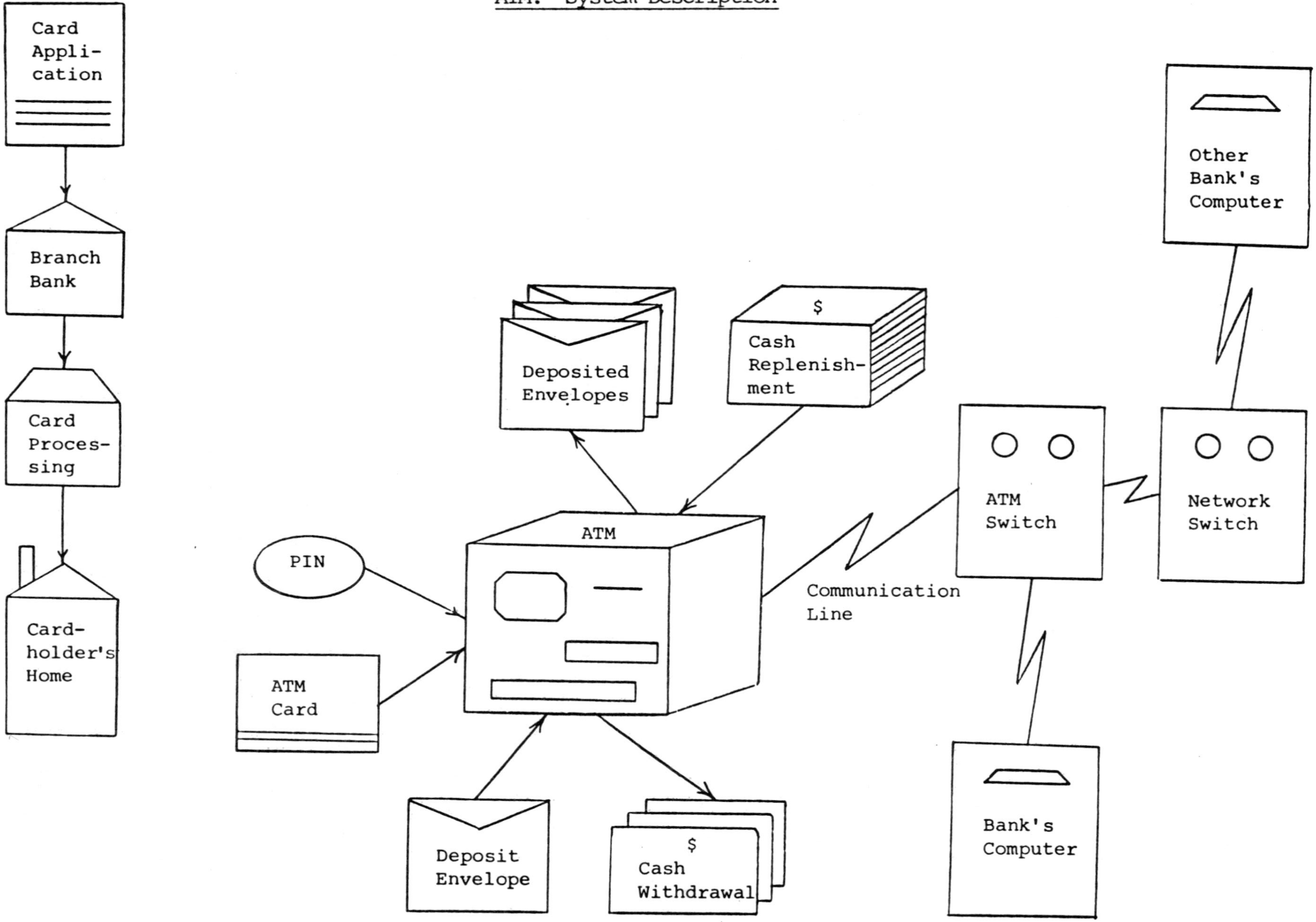

belongs to an accountholder of a network affiliate; it then routes the card information to the network switch which in turn routes the information to the user's financial institution's computer. The transaction is then processed as described above. As discussed in the next subsection, several factors provide impetus to financial institutions to form or join ATM networks; whatever the reason, the number of ATM networks has increased rapidly in the past five years. The number of shared regional networks, as of September 1984, is estimated at 175 [Bank Network News, 1984]. In addition, eight national ATM networks are operational. Not only are the number of networks increasing, but cardholders' use of networks is also increasing. A recent Bank Administration Institute (BAI) survey [1985] indicated that the number of interchange transactions (i.e., a transaction that occurred at an ATM not owned by the cardholder's financial institution) increased 27 percent from 1983 to 1984.

Customer acceptance of ATMs were at first slow, due in part to frequent malfunctions and the need to educate accountholders about this new technology. But since the late 1970's, ATM usage has dramatically increased. Exhibit 1.3 contains nationwide ATM statistics, estimated by one industry expert, L. F. Zimmer. Typically, as highlighted by Garsson [1983], Zimmer's estimates are higher than those of another industry expert, H. S. Nilson. We should note from Exhibit 1.3 that the number of installed ATM increased over three fold from 1980 to 1984. Will this trend continue? Probably not. Even though the total number of ATM transactions (i.e., withdrawals and deposits) has increased, the number of transactions per ATM has begun to decrease, suggesting that perhaps the country is beginning to reach a saturation point in ATM deployment.

Point-of-Sale (POS)

POS terminals are remote terminals that link a retail store to one or more financial institutions and allow customers to use a plastic, magnetically-encoded card -- not unlike an ATM card --to make purchases. When making a purchase, the customer slides the card through a small terminal, and enters his/her PIN. After the store employee enters the amount of the transaction, the terminal transmits this information to both the customer's financial institution and the store's financial institution. The customer's account is then debited, while the store's account is credited. The use of POS in this regard epitomizes the idea of the cashless, checkless society. In addition to direct debit, POS terminals can also be used for check authorization, check verification, and balance inquiries.

POS terminals offer several advantages to retail establishments. Operating costs can be reduced by the reduction of check and credit card processing expenses, the reduction of bad check losses, and the elimination of credit card and check "float" time. On the other hand, one problem that has occurred with some POS systems is that the communications network between retail stores and financial institutions has been limited. Often the system can only access the computer records of one financial institution; that is, only customers who bank at the single participating institution can use the POS system installed in the store. However, as noted earlier and as indicated in Exhibit 1.4, the growth of ATM networks is beginning to overcome this limitation. Indeed, despite some initial difficulties (i.e., networking issues concerning coordination of debit cards and ownership of the related hardware, software and switch; pricing decisions among the issuing bank, the consumer, the acquiring bank, and the retailer; technical limitations of available ATM switches which may be unable to handle the expected high POS volume at peak shopping hours; and marketing incentives for encouraging consumer acceptance of POS), POS is becoming a direct-debit service which is destined to change the way retailers of all kinds accept payment [Bergen, 1984; Myers, 1984].

Around the country, ATM networks now have electronic access to a majority of consumer deposit accounts at local banks and thrifts, and they are in a position to offer the retailer the broad card base that makes direct-debit POS a viable and lower-cost proposition than either checking or the manually processed credit cards. Even for retailers who now reject those high-cost forms of payment, the electronic debit card will offer a convenient and cost-effective alternative to cash. In sum, whereas ATM usage seems to be leveling off (at least on a per machine basis), POS usage is beginning to increase rapidly, perhaps mirroring the ATM growth of five years ago. According to one industry source [Bank Network News, 1985], 2,500 POS terminals were installed by the end of 1984, primarily at supermarkets and gas stations, while more than 25,000 are predicted to be installed by the end of 1985.

Home Banking

As the third major retail EFT technology, home banking allows accountholders to access their account records and initiate financial transactions (e.g., make loan or mortgage payments, transfer funds between accounts, or instruct the bank to pay merchants and utility companies) at home by using a touch-tone telephone, a TV monitor connected to a control box, or a personal computer terminal. The first home banking system simply involved the accountholder phoning the financial institution and giving verbal instructions to an employee. With the advent of the touch-tone telephone, information -- such as instructions to pay bills -- could be keyed directly to the bank's computer. Personal computers offer additional features that have increased the appeal of home banking. For example, accountholders can access special home banking software that provides user-friendly transaction menus, not unlike those displayed at ATMs. The proliferation of personal computers has prompted banks to market personal computer-based home banking systems, as opposed to the more cumbersome telephone-based systems.

As is the case of POS, personal computer-based home banking, while basically still in the pilot phase today, has recently experienced rapid growth. Moreover, this

5

Exhibit 1.3

ATM: Nationwide Statistics

	1978	1980	1982	1984
Installed ATMs (Year End)	9,750	18,500	35,721	58,470
Number of Transactions* Per Year	0.5 Billion	--	2.9 Billion	3.7 Billion
Dollar Volume of Transactions* Per Year	--	--	$241.4 Billion	$272.0 Billion

<u>Sources</u>: Zimmer [1979], [1981], [1983], [1985]

*Include only withdrawals and deposits.

Exhibit 1.4

POS: ATM Networks With POS Involvement

Name	Background	POS Involvement
PULSE	• Based in Texas, the network is a non-profit organization. • Largest regional ATM network.	• As Texas law requires mandatory sharing for all off-premise ATM and POS terminals, the network requires all member financial institutions to participate in POS.
Cirrus System Inc.	• Nationally based, the network began operation in January 1983. • Largest national ATM network with 1,036 member financial institutions, 5300 ATMs in 40 states, 15 million card holders, and processing 100,000 ATM transactions per month.	• Network plans to begin POS direct debiting by mid-1985 on a regional basis, most likely in California • (i.e., First Interstate Bank of California) and/or Texas (i.e., MPACT network).
Honor	• Based in Florida, the network has 305 member financial institutions and 4 million cardholders.	• Beginning with 30 stores (i.e., Crown Liquor stores, car dealers, convenience stores) in 1984, the network expects to expand to 1,000 outlets by early 1985.
MPACT	• Based in Dallas, the network is bank-owned. • Network has 825 ATMs and 3 million cardholders, and processes 5 million ATM transactions per month.	• Network has several hundred POS terminals (i.e., in Mobil, Shell and Exxon service stations and Tom Thumb stores).
Northwest Electronic Network	• Based in Seattle, the network is owned by 5 large banks.	• Network plans to begin POS in the second quarter of 1985.
Tyme	• Network is based in Milwaukee.	• Network has Atalla/POS terminals at Pick'n Save grocery stores.
Iowa Transfer System	• Based in Des Moines, Iowa (which law requires mandatory sharing of all off-premise ATM and POS), the network began operation in 1981. • Network has 905 member financial institutions and 800,000 cardholders.	• Network is the oldest fully-shared POS network — since 1981 — with terminals in two large supermarket chains (i.e., By-Vee and Dahl's).
Interlink	• Based in California, the network began operation in January 1985 with a 9 million card base and is owned by 5 large banks (i.e., First Interstate, Bank of America, Crocker, Security Pacific, and Wells Fargo), although other banks can join as non-equity participants.	• Network does not handle ATM transactions; it is devoted exclusively to POS transactions.
BUYPASS	• Network is based in Atlanta.	• Network has several hundred POS terminals.

growth is expected to continue. A recent survey [Tyson, 1985] estimated the number of users in mid-1985 to be 58,000, up from 44,000 in January 1985.

Corporate EFT Technologies

Less visible to the public than the retail EFT technologies, corporate EFT technologies use electronic communications to make instutition-to-institution or institution-to-consumer money transfers. The most dominant of these services is wire transfer, generally used by corporations to make large payments to other firms and individuals. (Although this study focuses only on wire transfers made through financial institutions, it is recognized that insurance companies, brokerage houses, retail stores, and other businesses may employ internal communications systems to route wire transfer-related messages.) Two other important yet much less widely used corporate EFT technologies are automated clearing houses (a service used primarily for direct deposit of payroll and government checks) and cash management services (which allow corporate customers to directly access records and initiate transactions through their own computer terminals). These three technologies are discussed below.

Wire Transfer

As the primary corporate EFT technology, wire transfer networks allow large dollar value transfers between and among financial institutions, the Federal Reserve, corporations, and private customers. Unlike the retail EFT technologies discussed above, wire trasnfer networks have been in operation for several decades, beginning with the Federal Reserve Board's installation in 1918 of a private Morse code telegraph system. As depicted in Exhibit 1.5, the wire transfer system facilitates the transfer of money from one party, called the originator or sender, to another party, called the beneficiary or receiver. The party might be an individual (e.g., a parent wishing to wire money to a child who is attending school), a corporation (e.g., a company wishing to transfer funds to one of its offices in another state), a bank (e.g., a bank wishing to transfer a large sum of money from one of its accounts to another bank's account), or any other organization. Depending on the sender, the transfer could be initiated in a number of ways. An individual could contact the bank by mail, messenger, telephone, or in person (i.e., over the counter). A large corporation has the capability to initiate wire transfers using TELEX, TWX, facsimile transmission, or the cash management technology that is discussed later. On the other hand, a large bank could initiate a transfer either through its own computer or one of the following four major wire transfer networks:

(1) FedWire. It is a private wire network operated by the Federal Reserve System to provide communications facilities among Fed district banks, financial institutions maintaining Federal Reserve accounts, and, as a result of the Monetary Control Act of 1980, all other depository institutions. A true payment network, FedWire accomplishes an immediate transfer, or settlement, of funds between the sending and receiving banks' accounts maintained at the Federal Reserve. In this manner, FedWire acts as a clearinghouse for wire transfer activity. In 1969, the Culpeper Switch became operational, providing computerzied communications between district banks. Previously, the Federal Reserve operated a teletype network. In 1981, more than 800 financial institutions were FedWire users via terminal or direct computer connections; the remaining banks used the telephone or other means to initiate transfers.

(ii) BankWire. Developed by its parent company, Payment and Telecommunications Services Corporation, BankWire is a private sector data communications network that links participating members of the banking industry and associated fields. Its primary purpose is to transmit funds and administrative information among its members. Unlike FedWire, BankWire does not act as a clearinghouse; debit and credit entries are made at the sending and receiving banks. The first BankWire teletype network was created in 1950. In mid-1974, the BankWire I computer system became operational; in May 1978, an enhanced network -- BankWire II -- was brought on-line. The enhanced network provides increased daily message volume capacity, greater system reliability, and standard message formats for funds transfers.

(iii) The Clearing House Interbank Payments Systems (CHIPS). It is operated by the New York Clearing House Association and was originally established to provide a system for the automation of interbank payments within New York City. Initially, its operation was confined to transfers of funds for international customers of member banks of the Clearing House; subsequently, other New York banks, both domestic and foreign, were allowed to participate in the network. As is indicated by its name, CHIPS acts as a clearinghouse, providing same day settlement for member banks.

(iv) The Society for Worldwide Interbank Financial Telecommunications (SWIFT). It was formed in 1973 by major European, American, and Canadian banks as a cooperative society. The network provides structured message formats for a wide range of fund transfers and other international banking transactions; it began live operation in March 1977, and was introduced in the United States in September 1977. In February 1980, a major SWIFT switching center went into operation at Culpeper,

8

Exhibit 1.5

Wire Transfer: System Description

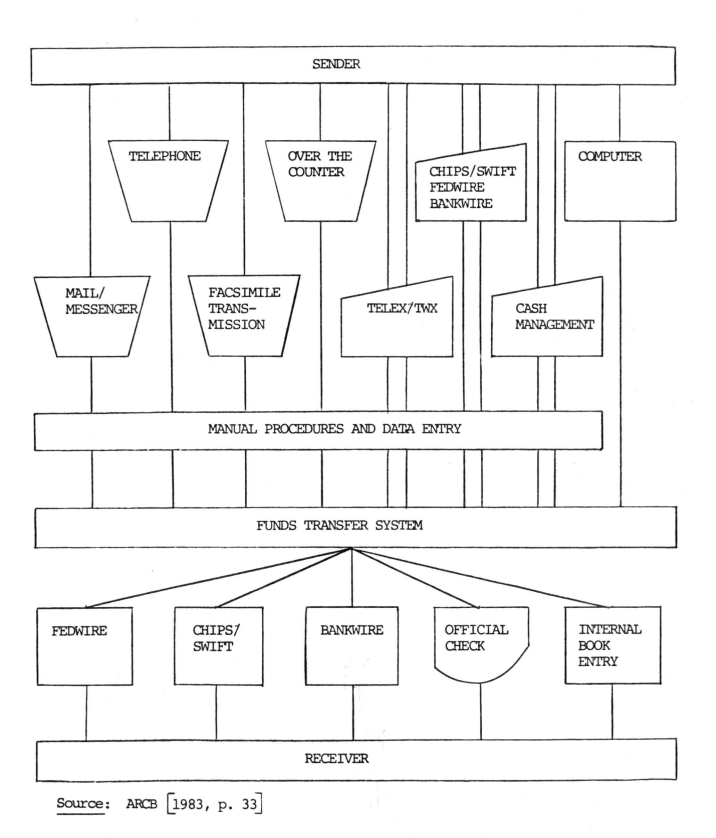

Source: ARCB [1983, p. 33]

Virginia. As of the first quarter in 1981, there were more than 900 member banks, including 111 U.S. members.

Referring to Exhibit 1.5, once the sender has initiated the wire transfer-related message, the bank processes the message (with possibly some manual intervention) through the fund transfer system. Information such as the beneficiary's name, the beneficiary's bank, the amount of the transfer is transmitted through the system. Specially designed software routes the message over communication lines -- typically through one of the four main networks described above -- on route to the beneficiary's bank, which then processes the incoming message and advises the beneficiary.

Wire transfers constitute the dominant form of non-cash transactions in the nation. As indicated in Exhibit 1.6, $668 billion was transferred per day over the CHIPS and FedWire networks in 1984. This dollar figure represents a 48.4 percent increase over that of 1980. Put another way, given a gross national product in 1984 of roughly $3.7 trillion, one might say that during the course of the year the GNP moved through the wire transfer system 47 times or once every 1.1 weeks!

Automated Clearing Houses (ACH)

The nation's 30 Automated Clearing Houses (ACHs) perform services similar to those provided by a manual check processing system. That is, an ACH gathers transaction data from various institutions, sorts it by the receiving institution, and then sends the information on to the receiving institution. The important difference is that the ACH performs these services electronically, using magnetic tapes. Additionally, as alluded to above, ACHs process transactions in "batch" mode, whereas ATM and POS systems generally operate in a "real-time", on-line mode. ACHs typically handle low value, repetitive dollar transfers such as direct deposit payroll or Social Security checks and preauthorized debit and bill payments. Whereas the average wire transfer is about $2 million, an ACH transaction averages less than $5,000.

Recently, however, the ACHs have experienced an increased growth. No longer primarily used for government-related transactions, ACHs are being used more and more by private organizations. Corporations, for example, see ACHs as a low cost alternative to the wire transfer networks [Ferris, 1985 (a)]. As shown in Exhibit 1.7, the annual dollar volume increased 68.3 times from 1980 to 1984.

Cash Management

Cash management services allow corporate customers to access their records electronically. In addition to accessing account balances, customers may transfer funds between accounts and initiate wire transfers. Just as home banking systems have benefited from increased use of personal computers in the home, cash management systems have grown in popularity alongside the increased use of office and business computers. Large banks are now aggressively marketing their proprietary computer-based "treasury workstations".

Internal EFT Technologies

Although to some, only those technologies that use electronic banking outside a financial institution's internal environment -- such as the retail and corporate technologies discussed above -- are accepted as EFT, a literal interpretation of "electronic fund transfer" also describes the computerized processing of checks, credit card purchases, and almost all of the transactions that occur in a financial institution. Indeed, computers are now firmly entrenched in the processing of virtually all financial transactions.

In sum, internal EFT technologies have and will continue to grow. The reasons for this growth center around the desire to perform financial transactions in a safer, more convenient, and more cost effective manner. Whereas increasing computer sophistication has been accompanied by decreasing computer costs, labor costs (especially those related to check processing and routine teller services) have been increasing steadily. This fact has become more important in recent years, as the banking industry becomes increasingly deregulated. Federal legislation in the early 1980s, especially the Monetary Control Act of 1980 and the Garn-St.Germain Depository Institutions Act of 1982, lifted many restrictions on banking activities and fueled increased competition in the banking industry. Competition has not only increased among banks, but also between banks and other providers of financial services such as brokerage houses, insurance companies, and even retail chains (e.g., Sears). Thus, in the internal banking sector, banks will continue to strive for lower operating costs through expanded use of EFT technologies.

1.2 EFT FRAUD

EFT fraud is but one type of computer crime. The focus of extensive public and media attention, computer crime has increased concomitant with the proliferation of computer use [Shea, 1984; Perry and Wallich, 1984]. As noted earlier, a recent study by the American Bar Association (ABA) [1984] considers computer crime to be a problem of substantial and growing significance. The ABA study, based on 283 responses to a survey mailing to approximately 1,000 private organizations and public agencies, revealed that computer crime is regarded as of equal or greater importance than many other types of white collar crime, including antitrust violation, counterfeiting, bank embezzlement, consumer fraud, securities fraud, and tax fraud.

Although much of the EFT abuse is sanctionable under existing criminal law, the law does not, for the most part, deal with such abuses. Thus, while theft statutes typically stipulate the taking of physical property, it must be asked whether the generation of an electronic signal, or the execution of a computer routine which changes an account balance, constitute "taking?" Do

10

Exhibit 1.6

Wire Transfer: Nationwide Statistics

	Number		Dollar Volume	
	1980	1984	1980	1984
Transactions				
FedWire	165,000[1]	160,000[2]	$308 Billion[1]	$368 Billion[2]
CHIPS	50,000[1]	90,000[3]	$142 Billion[1]	$300 Billion[3]
Messages				
SWIFT	238,500[1]	500,000[4]	--	--
BankWire	18,500[1]	Not Available	--	--

Sources: 1. Arthur D. Little [1982].
2. FedWire: Telephone conversation, June 7, 1985.
3. CHIPS: Telephone conversation, November 11, 1985.
4. SWIFT: Telephone conversation, June 7, 1984.

Exhibit 1.7

ACH: Nationwide Statistics

	1980[1]	1984[2]
Number of Transactions Per Day	895,400	2,303,800
Dollar Volume of Transactions Per Day	$0.15 Billion	$10.4 Billion

Sources: 1. Arthur D. Little [1982]
2. National Automated Clearing House Association: Telephone Conversation, June 7, 1985.

the contents of a computer memory constitute property? Further, fraud statutes require willful misrepresentation to a person -- are computers persons?

At present, as listed in Exhibit 1.8, there are 24 states which have computer crime statutes; however, only a few of these statutes specifically address EFT. At the federal level, the laws applicable to EFT crime or fraud include specific sections of the Electronic Funds Transfer Act of 1978 (which overlaps in the area of ATM disputes with the Federal Reserve Board's Regulation E), the wire fraud and mail fraud provisions of the Criminal Code, and the Counterfeit Access Device and Computer Fraud and Abuse Act of 1984. To date, there have been very few indictments -- much less convictions -- under any of these laws, making it difficult to predict how the courts may interpret these laws relative to EFT fraud.

Perhaps the current paucity of EFT-related crime laws is appropriate, as knowledge of the relationship between EFT and crime is sketchy at best. But as EFT technologies come to play an even more dominant role in the nation's payments system, criminal justice professionals will need to recognize the opportunities for and incidence of EFT-related criminal activities. Certainly, the results of this study should contribute to our knowledge of EFT fraud.

As EFT technologies proliferate, so does the potential for fraud. In fact, in regard to potential vulnerabilities in their ATM operations, bankers are especially sensitive about the growing fraud experiences of the credit card companies, especially in the area of card counterfeiting. Federal Regulation E (Reg E) has also increased the bankers' concern over ATM fraud as it limits cardholder liability [Ellis and Greguras, 1983], even when the cardholder is negligent. In the corporate banking area, the concerns are even greater, as enormous sums of money are transferred each day through the various wire transfer networks.

EFT fraud can assume one of many forms and the purpose of this section is to provide an overview of the key vulnerabilities to fraud in both the ATM and wire transfer systems. First, however, it is necessary to carefully define EFT fraud.

Definition of EFT Fraud

No commonly accepted definition of the term "EFT fraud" has emerged in the literature [Colton et al., 1982]. Nonetheless, the ability to differentiate frauds that can be attributed to the presence or operation of an EFT system from others that occur in financial institutions is a prerequisite for analyzing the nature and extent of EFT fraud. Ideally, a definition of EFT fraud should act like a sieve -- catching and identifying certain activities as EFT fraud while letting others slip through. Certain incidents clearly should be labeled EFT frauds. Withdrawals made using a stolen ATM card and alterations of a wire transfer by a bank employee for the purpose of improperly enriching an individual are certainly examples of EFT fraud. On the other hand, let us consider the following

incident, which occurred at a Midwest bank in 1984. A woman was making a withdrawal at an ATM located in a parking lot late at night. After completing the withdrawal, she was accosted by a man who had seen her perform the withdrawal. Using a gun, he ordered the woman to hand him the money that she had just withdrawn. Is this incident an EFT fraud (and therefore under the purview of Reg E)? Or, should it be considered traditional robbery?

In considering a definition of EFT fraud, it is important that the definition be sufficiently broad so that the impact of EFT technology on the incidence of fraud can be fully assessed. In particular, in this report, we adopt the definition advanced by Colton et al. [1982, p. 40] -- that is, EFT fraud is any crime, whether or not prosecuted under special computer/EFT laws or traditional law, that would not have occurred but for the presence of an EFT system. Under this definition, the robbery incident described above would be considered an EFT fraud, as the woman would not have been able to withdraw money from her account if it were not for the availability of an ATM. Interestingly, the Federal Reserve Board, the overseer of ATM-related regulations, recently ruled that if a consumer is forced by a robber to withdraw cash at an ATM, then "the actions of the robber are tantamount to use of a stolen access device" [EFTA, 1985(a)].

Potential for EFT Fraud

Armed with a definition of EFT fraud, we can now discuss the potential for EFT fraud, again focusing on the ATM and wire transfer technologies. Such a discussion provides an appropriate framework for considering our findings about ATM and wire transfer fraud in Sections 3 and 4, respectively. Of particular interest is the risk that each potential system vulnerability poses. Although many ATM frauds are likely to be attempted, and, if attempted, are likely to be successful, they typically result in small financial consequences or costs. An example would be a person who possesses a stolen ATM card and PIN; the person is not likely to withdraw more than a few hundred dollars before the card is "captured" by the ATM (i.e., "hotcarded"). On the other hand, although wire transfer frauds are unlikely to be attempted, and, if attempted, are unlikely to be successful, their financial costs could be staggering. (Note that in the wire transfer area, even if a fraudulent transfer is completed, the fraud cannot be considered successful until the money is withdrawn, a difficult undertaking if the sum of money is large.) The components of risk (i.e., likelihood, vulnerability, and cost) are further discussed in Section 5.2.

ATM

In the ATM area, there are a number of potential vulnerabilities (see Exhibit 1.9). (See also Boyle [1983].) Many of the vulnerabilities are associated with frauds perpetrated through the use of the ATM card, including both unauthorized use of an accountholder's card by others and fraudulent use by a legitimate cardholder. Some frauds do not involve the card directly, such as manipulation of the ATM system software, alteration of account information, and other

Exhibit 1.8

State-Level Computer Crime Statutes

	State	Year Statute Enacted
1.	Alaska	1983
2.	Arizona	1978
3.	California	1979
4.	Colorado	1978
5.	Delaware	1982
6.	Florida	1978
7.	Georgia	1980-81
8.	Illinois	1979
9.	Kentucky	1977
10.	Massachusetts	1983
11.	Michigan	1979
12.	Minnesota	1981-82
13.	Missouri	1983
14.	Montana	1981
15.	New Mexico	1979
16.	North Carolina	1980-81
17.	Ohio	1981-82
18.	Oklahoma	1984
19.	Pennsylvania	1984
20.	Rhode Island	1979
21.	Tennessee	1983
22.	Utah	1980-81
23.	Virginia	1978
24.	Wisconsin	1982

Exhibit 1.9

ATM: Potential Vulnerabilities

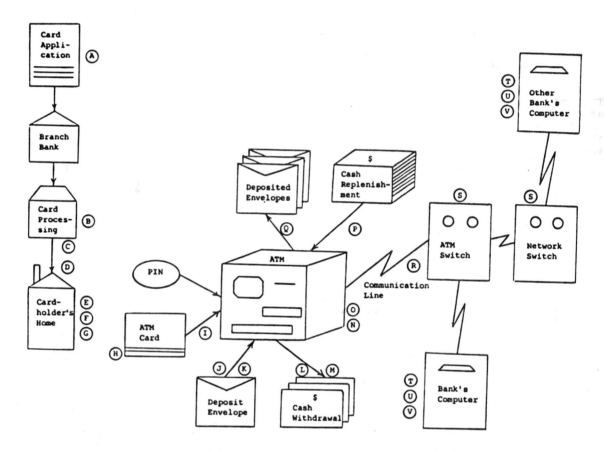

A. Account set up with intent to defraud
B. Card stolen from embossing vendor, processing center, or storage area
C. Theft of card and PIN from mail by postal employee
D. Theft of card and PIN from mailbox
E. Card stolen in burglary, larceny, or purse snap; card lost (PIN on or near card)
F. Unauthorized use by family, friend, or acquaintance
G. Misrepresentation of ATM transactions by cardholder
H. Alteration of magnetic stripe data
I. Active card left in machine; next person uses it to withdraw from cardholder's account
J. Empty envelope deposit followed by withdrawal, creating overdraft

K. Fraud check deposit followed by withdrawal against non-sufficient funds
L. Off-line overdraft by cardholder
M. False reporting that ATM did not dispense correct funds
N. Physical attack on ATM by outsider
O. Cardholder robbed leaving ATM
P. Replenishment cash subject to theft by service team member
Q. Theft of cash/checks from deposited envelopes
R. Electronic attack on data communication line
S. Manipulation of ATM processor software
T. Theft of account data
U. Manipulation of account/transaction data
V. System procedures allow one cardholder to remove cash from another's account

types of bank employee-related frauds. It should also be noted that aside from deliberate fraudulent acts, ATM systems are also vulnerable to inadvertent bank errors that may lead to the commission of fraud.

Perhaps the most familiar type of ATM fraud are those resulting from unauthorized use of an accountholder's card. Cardholders can lose possession of their card in a number of ways. The card could be stolen in the mail, from the person's wallet or purse, or obtained as the unanticipated byproduct of a burglary, street robbery or larceny. Cards can be taken by family members or friends or other persons who would have access to the cardholder's residence.

The individual who fraudulently obtains the card needs the PIN to activate the ATM, but as detailed in Section 3.2 and not surprisingly, the PIN is often written down by the cardholder and kept either on the card or on a separate piece of paper in the wallet or purse. PINs are also verbally revealed by accountholders, often in a casual manner to family members or friends. Accountholder negligence, however, is not always involved as PINs are also obtained forcefully, during a mugging attempt for example, or surrepticiously, as may be the case with confidence games.

Assuming the card and PIN are available to the unauthorized user, the financial consequences of this type of fraud depend on a number of factors. A daily withdrawal limit -- typically between $200 and $300 -- prevents excessive losses in any given day, but sometimes many days can pass before the accountholder becomes aware that his/her ATM card is missing and subsequently notifies the bank. Once notified, the bank can "hotcard" the missing ATM card, an action which captures the card the very next time it is used. Of course, unauthorized withdrawals might also be curtailed by a small account balance.

While it is the accountholder's funds that are being withdrawn, it should be noted that the bank is generally liable for any losses sustained by the accountholder. Reg E limits accountholder liability to $50 if the accountholder reports the card missing within two days of discovery, or $500 if the report is made more than two days after discovery. This liability ceiling is irrespective of accountholder negligence (e.g., even if the accountholder writes the PIN on the card).

Sometimes the financial consequences of a fraud are exacerbated by the user's ability to overdraw an account at an ATM. At some banks, ATMs are occasionally "off-line", meaning that the communication link between the ATM and the bank's computer is temporarily disconnected. If the ATM is off-line, an account balance "look up" may not be able to be made; consequently, the account may be overdrawn. Another vulnerability that allows users to overdraw an account are delayed withdrawal postings. Account balances, as "seen" by the ATM, may not reflect the true, up-to-the-minute balance; for example, a withdrawal made at a human teller may not be debited against the account balance until the end of the business day, during which time the ATM sees a balance that is greater than it should be.

Additionally, bad checks can be deposited in ATMs, accompanied by subsequent withdrawals that result in overdrafts. Of course, this scenario is not unique to the ATM environment. However, a special case of a bad deposit-related fraud --an "empty" deposit envelope (i.e., the user keys in a certain dollar deposit but intentionally does not place any cash or checks in the deposit envelope) -- is unique to ATMs.

ATM frauds are also committed by legitimate cardholders. The absence of sophisticated verification techniques (e.g., fingerprints or voiceprints) can provide unscrupulous cardholders with the opportunity to commit fraud from their own individual account. One common way is to misrepresent transactions. A cardholder can claim his card was stolen -- when in fact it was not -- or, even if the card was not missing, disclaim any knowledge of one or more withdrawals. Even if the ATM is equipped with a camera, this type of fraud is easy to perpetrate, since the cardholder can conspire with another person, who actually makes the withdrawals. Since Reg E places the burden of proof on the bank, it is often difficult to deny an accountholder's claim.

Non-card-related ATM fraud also occurs, as potential vulnerabilities to fraud exist in nearly every aspect of a highly complex banking operation like an ATM program. Cards may be taken from the mailing room or siphoned off from cards mailed and then "returned to sender" because of incorrect or out-of-date addresses. Cash may be stolen directly from the ATM replenishment canisters or the deposit envelopes by bank employees. Further, a range of electronic attacks can be made on the bank's computer system, including software alteration, fraudulent account creation, and removal of security controls on "hot" or blocked accounts. Compared to ATM card-related fraud, these and other types of employee fraud are potentially more serious in terms of their financial losses. At the same time, employee fraud occurs much less often than card-related fraud. Additionally, like a bank safe, the ATM can contain a large amount of cash and is therefore a target for robberies, sometimes requiring explosive means to gain entry [Matthews, 1983].

Inadvertent errors can also lead to the commission of a fraud. When processing withdrawals, ATMs can experience problems related to either dispensing (i.e., the wrong amount of funds is dispensed) or posting (i.e., the cardholder's account is not properly debited). Either of these events can lead to the improper enrichment of the cardholder. Similar malfunctions and errors, with potentially larger financial consequences, can also occur in deposit processing and, as discussed below, wire transfers.

Wire Transfers

Inasmuch as the wire transfer system involves multiple institutions and communication links, and serves to transfer payments on the order of millions of dollars each, there are many system vulnerabilities. The most prominent of these are identified in Exhibit 1.10 and can be classified according

15

Exhibit 1.10

Wire Transfer: Potential Vulnerabilities

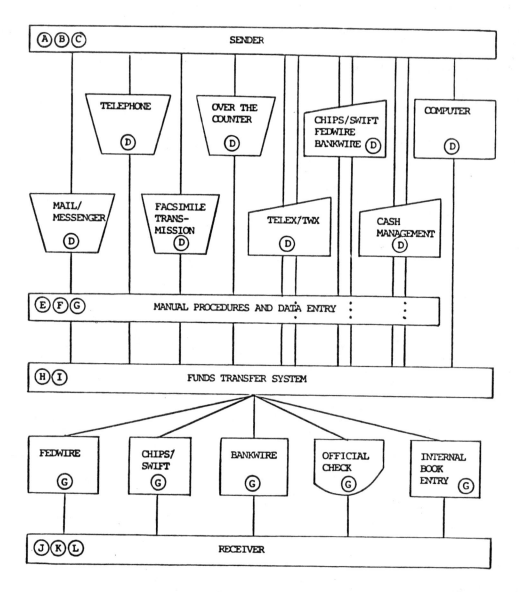

A. External Error in Message Initiation
B. Internal Error in Message Initiation
C. External Entry of Fraudulent Transaction
D. Internal Entry of Fraudulent Transaction
E. Bank Error in Message Content
F. Failure to Follow Established Procedures

G. Transaction Altered in Processing
H. Bank Error in Message Delivery
I. Purposeful Destruction of Transaction
J. Bank Error in Message Delivery
K. Bank Error in Customer Notification
L. Bank Error in Message Interpretation

to two generic types: inadvertent errors and intentional frauds. Each of these types is discussed below.

Errors made by corporate senders, clerks, computer terminal operators, or bank account officers can result in a wire transfer which is either for an incorrect amount, paid to the wrong beneficiary, or some combination thereof. The result of these and other inadvertent errors is often the sudden and improper enrichment of the individual or corporate beneficiary. Occasionally, the benficiary pockets all or part of the enrichment by physically absconding with the monies, refusing to return them on the grounds that they were owed the monies by the sender, or by feigning ignorance and spending the monies. Even when the bank which stands to sustain the loss recovers all or the majority of the principal, there can be associated costs such as legal fees, compensation or interest, and personnel time. Thus, an honest mistake can make possible the commission of a fraud -- perhaps by a heretofore honest beneficiary. Interestingly, some bank officials, while agreeing to the fact that the customer who absconds with the miscredited or double-credited money is commiting a fraud, view the act in a less severe light because, as one official puts it, "we gave him the opportunity to become a criminal."

Several types of inadvertant errors can occur. As displayed in Exhibit 1.10, errors can occur at all points in the wire transfer system, including at the point of initiation, in the manual procedures associated with the creation, processing and release of a message, and in the handling of the incoming message. These errors occur for a number or reasons. During a phone conversation with the sender, a clerk might record the wrong amount of money. Incoming messages -- especially if written in a foreign language or if the dollar amount is in a foreign currency -- can be misinterpreted. System failures, either with the bank's computer or the network's computer, can cause confusion as to which messages were and were not processed, possibly resulting in a duplicate payment. Finally, clerical errors, such a typographical error, can lead to improper enrichment.

The other type of wire transfer incidents, intentional frauds, include the initiation of an unauthorized wire transfer instruction either by an authorized bank official or by an outsider with knowledge of the procedures and codes required. Perhaps the most famous wire transfer fraud -- the $10.2 million Rifkin heist -- is an example of a fraudulent initiation of a wire transfer by an outsider. After having obtained the necessary codes surreptitiously, Rifkin impersonated an official at the bank to initiate a transfer. In addition to fraudulent transfer initiations, wire transfer messages can also be altered or destroyed by a perpetrator with a highly sophisticated knowledge of the data processing and telecommunications aspects of the wire transfer system. Given the increasing volume of wire transfer transactions and its enormous value, banks have sought to implement comprehensive and complex password, encryption and other hardware and software security measures to protect themselves from a big "hit".

1.3 STUDY BACKGROUND

In spite of both the phenomenal growth in the use of EFT systems and the increased concern for EFT-related fraud, there are no valid data on EFT fraud, as pointed out earlier. There are several reasons for this [Colton et al., 1982; Tien et al., 1984], including:

(i) the proprietary nature of EFT systems and the corresponding concern over potential competitive disadvantages that might result from the release of operational data;

(ii) the wide variations in definitions, procedures, and categories used by financial institutions to record transactions, fraud events, and charge-offs for sustained losses;

(iii) the technical and practical difficulties in identifying the occurrence of an EFT fraud, either while in progress or after the event;

(iv) the uncertainty about the legal status of specified actions that may (or may not) constitute a crime in a given jurisdiction;

(v) the common practice of handling EFT violations by in-house security or personnel procedures rather than by the standard criminal justice system;

(vi) the absence of a comprehensive or central data source -- like the FBI Uniform Crime Reports -- for capturing EFT data;

(vii) the nonexistence of a standardized and comparative data base against which EFT losses can be measured on a trend-line basis; and

(viii) the relatively recent development of EFT technologies, some of which are still in their initial implementation phases.

Nevertheless, despite the above cited difficulties, several attempts at collecting EFT fraud data have been made: four of those are discussed below.

SRI Study

This file originated in the early 1970s as the focus of a National Science Foundation sponsored study on computer crime (later, funding support was provided by the Justice Department). The study sought to identify computer crimes and to obtain some perception of their nature and extent [Parker and Nycum, 1979; Parker, 1980]. The file, an on-going compilation of over 1000 computer abuse cases identified through individual contacts and a newspaper clipping service, is the most well-known record of computer crime -- although it does not rely on any systematic or scientific data collection techniques.

The file focuses on computer abuse in general, rather than on EFT in particular; nevertheless, several of the cases from financial institutions were identified as being EFT-related. The file provides some information on the nature of computer crime, but is limited as a source of data to measure the extent of EFT fraud as it includes only those cases which were selected by the media or the researchers. For example, large losses or unique frauds were often brought to the attention of the researchers, although they obviously did not constitute a representative sample of all fraud cases. Compounding the problem is the fact that the EFT-specific frauds were not a primary focus of the SRI researchers, but a by-product of the collection effort. The file is a useful collection of cases, but it is not a statistically valid sample.

Federal Regulators

Until recently, all the federal regulatory agencies (i.e., Comptroller of the Currency, Federal Deposit Insurance Corporation, Federal Reserve Board, Federal Home Loan Bank Board) required financial institutions to report external (e.g., robbery, burglary) and internal (e.g., employee fraud, embezzlement) crimes. In general, the report consisted of a letter or a standard form which identified the apparent irregularity and briefly described the nature of the incident. These perfunctory reports typically provide minimal information.

Now, however, as a result of the paper-reduction emphasis in the Federal Government, a bank must report only internal crimes and maintain an informal, in-house record of each external crime. Consequently, information on external crimes at financial institutions are no longer available in a reasonably accessible form. Also, as the regulators use crime reports for specific and limited purposes, they are not collected or maintained in a manner which would make it easy to identify or aggregate EFT frauds.

Although the federal regulators are a potential source of data on EFT fraud, they cannot provide the relevant information without major policy and procedural changes. Not only would the reports on external crimes need to be reinstated, but the reporting forms would have to be significantly altered to allow for easy retrieval of data on EFT or computer crimes.

Federal Bureau of Investigation (FBI)

The FBI investigates most cases of bank fraud and embezzlement and maintains case records on federal offenses. (Note that financial crimes are considered federal offenses if the bank is federally-chartered or if bank assets cross state lines in the course of a criminal act.) Information on each case is recorded for historical and investigative purposes, and a variety of recordkeeping systems are maintained.

However, the FBI does not identify the use of a computer or an EFT technology in a case, mostly because it has no special bearing on broad law enforcement or prosecutorial efforts. In addition, although the FBI investigates the majority of financial crimes, records for many small bank crimes are usually maintained only at the local FBI office. Thus, the national FBI records omit many EFT frauds, while emphasizing large losses and complex scenarios. Further, the FBI has a policy against providing case information on a regular basis, and numerous regulations emphasize extreme confidentiality.

The recently enacted Counterfeit Access Device and Computer Fraud and Abuse Act of 1984 makes computer, as well as EFT, crimes a federal offense, thus bringing those acts under the purview of the FBI. However, the section of the Act applying to ATM fraud makes it a federal offense only if $1,000 or more was obtained during a 12-month period. Even if the FBI were to share this information, it obviously would not constitute a representative sample of ATM frauds.

American Institute of Certified Public Accountants (AICPA) Study

In 1979, the AICPA [1984] decided to examine computer fraud in hopes of establishing appropriate accounting and auditing standards. It approached the task on an industry-by-industry basis, starting with banking. In cooperation with the Bank Administration Institute (BAI), 9,000 commercial banks were selected to represent a geographic sample of the industry, and the sample was picked to assure that all of the major financial institutions were included.

However, the survey did not focus on the extent of computer fraud in banking. Rather, each institution was asked to describe only one case on the provided questionnaire. More than one-half of the sampled banks replied, although the vast majority indicated no computer fraud problems. Of the 5,000 responses, only 106 computer fraud cases were provided and only 85 were eventually classified as computer frauds. Unfortunately, although the study provides some information on the nature of EFT fraud, it cannot be used to statistically estimate the extent of fraud as it asked for only one example of an EFT or computer fraud, not the actual incidence of all such frauds.

1.4 SCOPE OF REPORT

This report is comprised of five major sections and one appendix. The first section provides important background information on EFT: the different technologies, the vulnerabilities to fraud, and the previous attempts to collect data.

Section 2 describes the approach taken in this study to assess the nature and extent of EFT fraud. Important study considerations are discussed in Section 2.1; highlights of the study conduct are contained in Section 2.2; and background information on the panel banks is detailed in Section 2.3.

Section 3, consisting of three subsections, addresses ATM fraud. The ATM-related data collection procedures are described in Section 3.1, while the nature and extent of ATM fraud are discussed in Section 3.2 and 3.3, respectively.

Wire transfer fraud is the subject of Section 4. The wire transfer-related data collection procedures are discussed first in Section 4.1, followed by an assessment of the nature of and the attitudes toward wire transfer fraud in Sections 4.2 and 4.3, respectively.

Section 5 concludes the report. After summarizing our key findings in Section 5.1, we present in Section 5.2 the concept of risk in the context of EFT fraud, together with an initial attempt at modeling risk. Other possible future efforts in the EFT fraud area are discussed in Section 5.3.

Finally, five exhibits are contained in Appendix A; they consist of the major data collection instruments used in the study. Where meaningful, the number of responses, as well as the resulting distribution and average or mean, are displayed on the exhibits in italics.

2 STUDY APPROACH

As summarized in Section 1.3, it was obvious that none of the available data sources on EFT fraud could provide valid data for measuring the nature and extent of EFT fraud. Each has only limited information, and all have problems from a statistical perspective. Further, although several offered a possible source of information, the potential existed only if major changes could be made in the collection processes --changes which seemed highly unlikely to occur. These sources offered perceptions or clues about the nature of EFT fraud, but did not provide an adequate data base for statistical analysis. It was further obvious that valid and consistent data could only be provided by the banks themselves.

To this end, we proposed to obtain EFT-related data directly from a small panel of commmercial banks. As detailed in Section 2.2, we were able to convene --with the help of the Association of Reserve City Bankers (ARCB) -- a panel of banks for our study. This Study Panel of 16 ARCB member banks has provided pertinent ATM and wire transfer fraud data for two years -- 1983 and 1984. Obtaining fraud data directly from the banks represents a major breakthrough. For many obvious reasons, banks are reluctant to share any information that might shake the consumer's confidence in the banking system. On the other hand, casting the few headline-capturing EFT fraud incidents in perspective and in relation to the total transaction volume is perhaps one reason 16 ARCB member banks -- out of a total of 18 invited banks -- agreed to participate in this study on an anonymous basis. Another reason is the knowledge provided by the study concerning EFT fraud, at both the individual bank level and the aggregate level. While data from a sample or panel of banks could provide a valid and on-going measure of the nationwide EFT fraud problem (in much the same manner that A.C. Nielsen Co. rates television programs based on data collected from a national panel of some 1,200 households), it is obvious that a 16-bank panel is inadequate for such a purpose -- it could not be representative of the more than 14,000 commercial banks. Consequently, the study documented herein represents a pilot effort and its findings should be regarded as preliminary.

The Study Panel approach has several advantages. First, it provides a "clean" source of data that could be used confidently to draw conclusions about the nature and extent of EFT fraud. Second, it allows for the acquisition of a consistent set of data so that such relative measures as the ratio of EFT fraud losses to total EFT transactions can be determined and then employed to estimate the national losses due to EFT fraud. Third, it sensitizes the banking industry not only to the actual EFT fraud problem but also to the need to develop valid and consistent measures of the problem. Fourth, if the Panel was to be enlarged and surveyed on an on-going basis, it would provide a continuing barometer of EFT fraud.

In order to convene the Study Panel and to collect consistent data from its members, we had to consider several issues: these are addressed in Section 2.1, followed by a synopsis of important study activities in Section 2.2 and a description of the Panel banks in Section 2.3.

2.1 STUDY CONSIDERATIONS

In our approach to assessing the nature and extent of EFT fraud, three critical issues had to be considered: (i) How could we secure the participation of financial institutions in our Study Panel? (ii) How large should the Panel be, given the scope of the study? and (iii) How can consistent data be collected from the Panel members? These three issues are considered below.

Panel Participation

Obviously, the success of this study depended on securing the participation of financial institutions in our Study Panel. However, the release of information about the incidence of bank fraud, particularly as it relates to white collar fraud, has been viewed as especially sensitive. In the increasingly competitive banking world, financial institutions avoid any events that could possibly shake the public's confidence in their industry. At the same time, however, bank officials have also been concerned that the public has misunderstood the nature and extent of EFT fraud, partly due to well-publicized "big hits" such as the Rifkin heist and the recently reported $40,000 theft from a Springfield (MA) ATM [Gallant, 1984]. Further, as bankers realize that little data now exist to support or refute assertions about the potential for EFT fraud, they understand the utility -- both in terms of public opinion and their own internal evaluations and decisions regarding EFT -- of obtaining better information so that EFT can be viewed from a realistic perspective. Thus, in our attempt to secure a bank's participation in our study, we emphasized the study's contribution to both the industry and the individual Panel members.

Additionally, in order to increase the likelihood that a selected financial institution would participate in a national panel, it was also clear that some form of co-sponsorship with an established banking-related organization would be helpful. Specifically, it was hoped that the co-sponsoring organization could secure the backing of the senior management of the participating financial institution.

Also, we knew that participation in the Panel would be enhanced if strict confidentiality were a condition of participation. All members of the Panel would need to be assured that the data collected from their individual institutions could never be directly identified with them. Thus, all findings and statistics would have to be reported in an aggregate or merged fashion across all the participating banks. In this manner, the identity of any member of the Panel could not be deduced from the published findings.

Panel Size

Whereas a telephone- or mail-based survey can sample a large number of financial institutions, the Study Panel approach precluded a large sample size because of the necessary and intensive interaction that would be required, including periodic site visits, with the participating financial institutions. Because of resource --time and cost -- constraints, we projected that the Study Panel should consist of 12 member banks.

Again, as indicated earlier, such a small number of banks cannot be representative of the more than 14,000 commercial banks in the U.S. Indeed, this study represents only a pilot test of the Study Panel approach and any resultant findings should be regarded as preliminary.

Consistent Data

Assuming a Study Panel could be formed, a larger question remained: Could consistent data be collected from the participants? For the purpose of data collection, an ideal situation would be one in which detailed records of all the EFT fraud incidents -- segregated by technology -- were kept in a single "file cabinet" and all associated fraud losses were charged to a single account. We knew, however, that this would not be the case in most financial institutions, as it is often difficult for bank investigators to determine whether an EFT incident actually involves a fraud. As pointed out in Section 1.2, ATM incidents involving disputed withdrawals by the accountholder may be caused by an unauthorized person fraudulently using the card, by the accountholder who is trying to defraud the bank, or by forgetfulness on the part of the accountholder. In many cases, the financial institution cannot determine the true cause and therefore whether to label the complaint as a fraud. As another example, a wire transfer request that is rejected because it does not meet certain procedural requirements may actually be a purposeful, yet unsuccessful, fraudulent act. Thus, a financial institution's "pool" of records of frauds depends to a large extent on subjective judgements.

A second "threat" to consistency concerns the handling of those incidents identified by the financial institution as fraud-related. Is documentation of the incidents maintained long after the incident occurred? Moreover, is the documentation sufficiently detailed? If not, then a retrospective data collection effort would not be feasible, and incidents may have to be collected on an on-going, prospective basis. Summary figures for fraud loss are also subject to inconsistencies, especially if they are pooled with other types of losses such as non-fraud losses, other non-EFT fraud losses, or other "miscellaneous" losses.

Data consistency can undoubtedly be enhanced by the use of specially-designed questionnaires or data collection instruments. Incident forms that are, for example, tailored to extract information from existing bank records -- or, alternatively, to record information as the incident occurs -- should help in this regard. Data consistency can be further enhanced if we, as data analysts, were to do all the coding; this would allow for consistency of interpretation. On the other hand, it would require that copies of the original source documents be forwarded to us and that we undertake a massive coding effort. For the sake of data consistency, we did indeed develop special data collection instruments (some of which are contained in Appendix A) and code most of the incident-level data ourselves.

2.2 STUDY CONDUCT

Exhibit 2.1 lists the 9 major study activities reported herein; they are shown in terms of a 21-month time line. Each of these activities is discussed below.

Study Panel

As noted in Section 2.1, in order to increase the likelihood of participation among financial institutions, some form of co-sponsorship with an established, banking-related organization was needed. Fortunately, as indicated earlier, the ARCB [1983] had recently completed a study of the nation's payment systems and had come to the conclusion "that the ARCB should support a study of the nature and frequency of fraud in these systems and explore ways in which meaningful information regarding fraud losses may be collected, analyzed, and disseminated to participants." Thus, we entered into a cooperative relationship with the ARCB; they sponsored our study among their membership and we undertook the work. Additionally, a confidentiality agreement was reached with the ARCB wherein we agreed to ensure the anonymity of the Study Panel members and to allow the ARCB to review -- from an anonymity perspective --all reports prior to publication.

In several respects, the ARCB has been an ideal co-sponsor of this study. First, as noted above, the ARCB -- through its own Risk Task Force -- saw a need for such a study. Second, the ARCB membership consists of the Chairmen of the Boards of some 200 of the largest commercial banks in the U.S. These large banks are in fact the prime movers in the developing EFT field, as few small financial institutions can justify extensive EFT systems. Third, in its typically progressive manner, the ARCB has been totally supportive of all aspects of the study; indeed, we wish to formally acknowledge their unwavering assistance and support.

Following the identification of the ARCB as the co-sponsor of the study, the question remained as to which of the ARCB member banks should be selected and solicited to join our Study Panel. One obvious consideration was that all Panel members should have extensive experience in EFT systems. Again, this experiential requirement was not a problem for most ARCB member banks, as they have mature ATM systems and direct access to one or more of the main wire transfer networks. To facilitate the selection of potential Panel members, we compiled an extensive data base on the nation's major banking institutions, as reflected in the ARCB membership. Drawing from annual reports and various banking

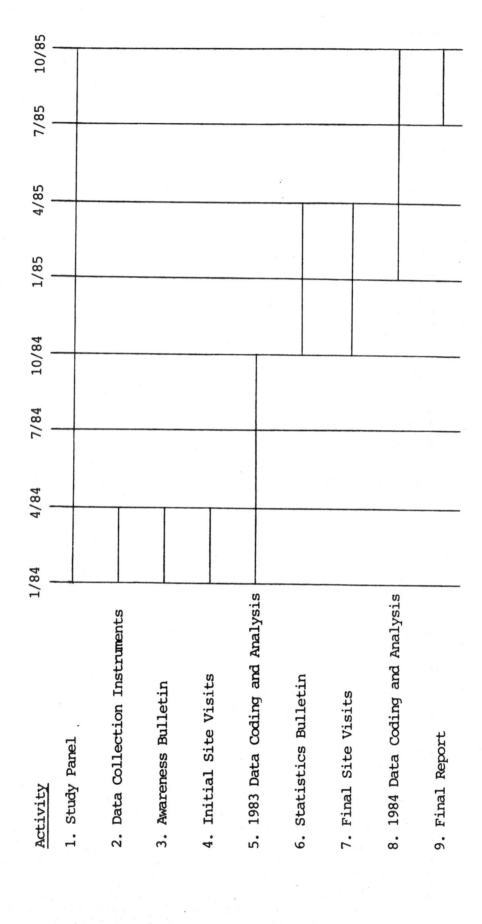

Exhibit 2.1

Major Study Activities and Schedule

Activity

1. Study Panel

2. Data Collection Instruments

3. Awareness Bulletin

4. Initial Site Visits

5. 1983 Data Coding and Analysis

6. Statistics Bulletin

7. Final Site Visits

8. 1984 Data Coding and Analysis

9. Final Report

1/84   4/84   7/84   10/84   1/85   4/85   7/85   10/85

22

journals and newsletters, information was collected on a bank's general background (e.g., assets, deposits, number of branches, holding company information, location), retail EFT activity (e.g., number of ATMs, year first ATM was installed, national and regional ATM network affiliations, POS services, and home banking systems), and corporate EFT activity (e.g., wire transfer, ACH, and cash management services). Given this information and working with the ARCB, we selected 18 banks (representative of the ARCB membership), hoping that 12 of them would agree to participate in the Study Panel and to provide fraud-related data for the calendar years 1983 and 1984. Subsequently, the ARCB wrote to the Chairmen of these 18 banks to solicit their banks' participation in the Study Panel. Surprisingly, all but two of the 18 banks agreed to participate; their only conditions for participation were that (i) their participation be kept confidential, and (ii) all published data would be in aggregate form, reflecting the experience of the entire Study Panel. Although the other two banks expressed interest in the study and were supportive of the study goals, they were unable to commit the time necessary to actively participate in the study. Given the unexpected level of positive responses, we agreed with the BJS monitor for this study that the Study Panel be expanded to include the 16 banks. (Some characteristics of these 16 banks are discussed in Section 2.3.)

The interest shown by the invited ARCB banks and the extremely high yield demonstrate that financial institutions view the lack of EFT fraud data as a serious problem and are willing to commit time and effort toward remedying that deficiency. Additionally, the evidence clearly indicates that a larger panel of banks could be convened, if it were desirable.

Finally, as indicated in Exhibit 2.1, we maintained contact with the member banks of our Study Panel throughout the study period. Additionally, although the Panel has never met as a group, individual Panel members have contacted each other to discuss matters of mutual interest.

Data Collection Instruments

For both the ATM and wire transfer areas, we collected three types of data: incident, summary, and background data. In addition, in order to supplement the Panel banks' wire transfer related data, we conducted a nationwide survey of wire transfer managers -- in particular, we were interested in their attitudes concerning fraud. For each type of data, we developed a special data collection instrument -- five such instruments are contained in Appendix A.

Developing an instrument that adequately captures the important information about a particular area of interest was a difficult task. Indeed, the instruments were basically developed from scratch, with some help from bank contacts, industry experts, and our review of currently existing forms. Once a draft version was prepared, it required testing on actual data to discover its shortcomings. This iterative process of testing and re-developing continued until the

final version was agreed upon. Further details regarding the development of the ATM and wire transfer instruments are in Sections 3.1 and 4.1, respectively.

The various instruments were distributed to the key ATM and wire transfer bank contacts when we visited the banks. While we explained to the bank contacts that the primary goal of the instruments was to extract already existing information, we also emphasized that the instruments, in particular the ATM and wire transfer forms, were also developed from an operational perspective, in the sense that they could be used by the banks for their own administrative and investigative purposes. It was our feeling that if the banks were to adopt our developed forms, then the resultant data would be both more accurate and already coded for analysis. Some of the Panel banks are seriously considering integrating one or more of our forms into their system, especially since the forms can be straightforwardly implemented on a computer. Indeed, for our own coding and analysis purposes, we have worked with computer-based versions of our developed instruments.

Awareness Bulletin

As a way of increasing public awareness of EFT fraud, preliminary study findings were disseminated to both the public and the greater banking community. The first of several study products was what we refer to as an EFT Awareness Bulletin [Tien et al., 1984], published by the BJS in February 1984 in their Special Report Series. Entitled "Electronic Fund Transfer and Crime", the Bulletin provided an overview of fraud-related issues in EFT. Specifically, the Bulletin identified potential areas for criminal abuse; noted how crime concerns have heightened as the use of EFT systems has grown; and discussed issues related to the collection of valid data on EFT fraud.

Reflecting the national interest in EFT in general, and EFT fraud in particular, the Awareness Bulletin, even though it contained no actual EFT fraud data, received coast-to-coast coverage and was quoted in all three communications media (i.e., print, radio, and video).

Initial Site Visit

One of our most important study activities was the initial site visit to each one of our Panel banks. In the participation acceptance letter to the ARCB, the Chairman of each Panel bank designated a key bank officer -- usually a senior vice president -- to be our bank contact. The initial site visit to each Panel bank was arranged and coordinated by this contact. Typically, we spent one day at each bank. The day began with a meeting with the bank contact for the purpose of introducing ourselves and discussing the scope of our study. We particularly stressed our commitment to maintaining confidentiality. Later, meetings were arranged with both managerial and operations personnel from the ATM, wire transfer, audit, and security departments of the bank. During these meetings, we focused on accomplishing two main objectives. The first involved understanding the bank's EFT operations from both an operations and a risk-to-fraud perspective. Of particular importance was understanding how fraud incidents are investigated, where their records were being maintained, and what types of summary reports were being generated. The second objective concerned our data requests for the year 1983. More specifically, we discussed our data collection instruments, determined the number of incidents to be included in the bank's 1983 data sample, and established procedures for the bank to provide us with the requested data.

Discussions with the bank contacts did not end after the site visits. As mentioned earlier, one of the factors contributing to the unavailability of valid data on EFT fraud is the wide variety of definitions, procedures, and categories used by financial institutions to record transactions, fraud events, and charge-offs for sustained losses. Inevitably, problems arose regarding our data requests. For example, one or more data elements or types of incidents might not have been collected by the bank. Or, if the requested data were available, they might have been in a slightly different format. The data also might not have been accessible from a logistical point of view. Additionally, changes in bank personnel presented problems of continuity. Although these and other complications required extensive follow-up contact with each bank, including frequent telephone conversations and additional site visits, the continuing interaction between ourselves and our bank contacts enhanced the consistency and validity of the obtained data.

1983 Data Coding and Analysis

After our initial site visits, the banks acted on our data requests in as expeditiously a manner as possible, given their normal day-to-day workload. We received the 1983 data over a period of several months. Unfortunately, due to time constraints, a "cut-off date" of September 30, 1984, had to be enforced, at which time no further 1983 data could be included in the analysis. To facilitate the analysis of the ATM and wire transfer incidents, we coded the incident records and entered them into a sophisticated data base management system that had been specially tailored to reflect the unique characteristics of the incident records. The resultant ATM and wire transfer incident analyses are discussed in Sections 3.2 and 4.2, respectively. It should be noted that the coding and analysis of the incident records have been quite time consuming; as indicated in Exhibit 2.1, this activity has been carried out over a period of 9 months.

Although not as time consuming as in the case of incident records, the coding and analysis of the summary loss data for ATM and the attitudinal survey data for wire transfer have also been extensive; the resultant analyses are discussed in Sections 3.3 and 4.3, respectively.

Statistics Bulletin

Referred to as the Statistics Bulletin [Tien et al., 1985], this product, entitled "Electronic Fund Transfer Fraud", was prepared in late 1984 -- based on the aforementioned analysis of 1983 data -- and published in the BJS Special Report Series in March 1985. Inasmuch as this Bulletin was the first ever to contain statistically valid data on EFT fraud, it surpassed the Awareness Bulletin in capturing the attention of the public, the media, and the banking community. The Statistics Bulletin was featured on national morning and evening television news programs, as well as radio, newspapers, and financial dailies --e.g., Weinstein [1985(a)]. Indeed, the BJS study monitor was interviewed by several news and talk show hosts, and was invited to join a special panel on "EFT Crime and Security", chaired by the Assistant Secretary of Electronic Systems and Information Technology, U.S. Department of The Treasury.

Results contained in the Statistics Bulletin were presented at key meetings and conferences. As discussed in Section 4.3, some results -- in particular, the wire transfer-related findings -- were presented to an enthusiastic audience at the 1984 Money Transfer Developments Conference in Chicago, sponsored by the Bank Administration Institute (BAI). In June 1985, we were invited to address the Eastern Regional Retail Services Convention, sponsored by the American Bankers Association (ABA). In general, reaction to our findings at these and other gatherings has been extremely positive. The dearth of EFT fraud data to this point has prompted an intense public interest in our results, and a desire in the banking community to expand our limited data collection effort. As one banker states it, "For once, we have some real numbers -- I'm using them to make my decisions on EFT services."

Final Site Visits

Our final round of site visits was carried out for two reasons. First, we wanted to share our analysis of the 1983 data and to have the benefit of the bank's reactions to the analysis. Not surprisingly, our analysis results were enthusiastically received. The banks were particularly interested in comparing their fraud-related experiences with those of the Study Panel, since in most cases one bank is unaware of the nature of the fraud occurring at another bank, even though both may be victims of the same or similar acts of fraud.

Our second reason for visiting the Panel banks was to solicit their participation in providing us with 1984 data. Given their positive reaction to our analysis of their 1983 data, the Panel banks, were, for the most part, very willing to share their 1984 data.

1984 Data Coding and Analysis

Similar types of coding and analysis were performed on the 1984 data as were performed on the 1983 data. As before, it was necessary to abide by a cut-off date; in this case, because of the end-of-study date of September 30, 1985, the cut-off date had to be June 30, 1985 -- as a result, less data was received for 1984 than for 1983.

It should be noted that the additional year's data allowed for a better understanding of EFT fraud, a by-product of simply increasing the amount of data. Additionally, some trend information was obtained. The two years of ATM data were analyzed separately, as documented in Sections 3.2 and 3.3. However, as detailed in Section 4.2, the small number of wire transfer incidents precluded a year-by-year analysis.

Final Report

The final study activity has involved assembling all the collected and analyzed data and presenting it in an informative and readable manner, as contained in this Final Report.

2.3 Panel Characteristics

Recognizing that our confidentiality agreement with the ARCB precludes detailed descriptions of the Study Panel members, we provide in this section only summary characteristics of the Panel.

As stated in Section 2.2, all of the Panel banks are commercial banks whose Chairmen belong to the ARCB. None of the other types of financial institutions involved with EFT, such as savings and loan institutions, mutual savings banks, or credit unions, are represented in the Panel. Moreover, as illustrated in Exhibit 2.2(a), all of the Panel banks have assets greater than $1 billion. In contrast, only 1.8 percent of the 14,473 FDIC-insured commercial banks have assets greater than $1 billion. This comparison is somewhat misleading, since -- as noted in Exhibit 2.2(a) -- these large banks control 56.7 percent of all the assets. Moreover, these same banks probably control nearly all of the deployment and use of EFT technologies, which constitute the focus of our study. Nevertheless, we certainly cannot claim that the 16-member Study Panel is representative of all commercial banks, much less of all financial institutions. This fact is the key reason why our study should only be considered a pilot effort.

In many respects, however, the Study Panel is representative. It is representative of the ARCB membership, for example. Geographically, all regions of the U.S. are included in the Panel: 4 banks are located in the Northeast, 5 in the South, 4 in the Midwest, and 3 in the West. More importantly, as noted earlier, the Study Panel's EFT operations can be considered to be somewhat representative of all EFT systems in the nation. Surprisingly, the average number of transactions (i.e., withdrawals and deposits) per ATM per month is lower than many of the widely-quoted industry averages: in 1983, for example, Zimmer [1984], in her annual report on ATMs, estimated an average monthly financial transaction value of 6,500 per ATM, of which 95 percent, or 6,175, were deposits or withdrawals, a figure significantly higher than the Panel bank average of 3,572 + 578 = 4,150 in that same year -- see Exhibit 2.2(b). At the same time, however, the average withdrawal and deposit amounts at the Panel banks -- $46 and $428 in 1983, respectively -- are higher than Zimmer's [1984] figures of $37 and $300, respectively. The 1983 to 1984 changes in Exhibit 2.2(b) for the various ATM statistics of the Panel banks are also reflective of industry-wide trends of growing numbers of installed ATMs and decreasing per machine volumes. Regarding experience in the ATM area, the Panel banks first installed ATMs, on the average, in 1976.

Finally, in the wire transfer area, the Panel banks processed an average of 3,343 transactions per day in 1983. This figure increased 7.9 percent in 1984, again indicative of industry wide trends. The average dollar amount per transfer in 1983 was $1.12 million, which increased 9.4 percent (to $1.23 million) in 1984.

25

Exhibit 2.2

Study Panel Characteristics

Asset Range ($ Billions)	Panel Banks	All FDIC Insured Commercial Banks	
	Column Percent (N=16)	Percent of Total Banks (N=14,473)	Percent of Total Assets (N=$2.03 Trillion)
< $1.0	0.0%	98.2%	43.2%
$1.0-$5.0	31.2	1.4	20.9
> $5.0	68.8	0.4	35.9
Total	100.0%	100.0%	100.0%

Source: FDIC [1984]

(a) Assets As of 12/31/83

	Number 1983/1984	Percent Charge
Installed ATMs (Average)	128/146	+13.8%
Withdrawals Per ATM Per Month	3,522/3,452	-2.0%
Deposits Per ATM Per Month	578/566	-2.0%
Average $ Withdrawal	$46/$48	+5.0%
Average $ Deposit	$428/$437	+2.0%

(b) ATM Statistics

3 ATM FRAUD

As suggested by the title of this report, our approach to assessing ATM fraud has been two-pronged. On the one hand, we have been interested in the nature of ATM fraud: What are the common types of fraud? What are their causes? Who are the perpetrators? On the other hand, while an analysis of the nature of ATM fraud addresses these and other related issues, such an analysis does not address important questions concerning the extent of ATM fraud, including: What are the projected nationwide losses due to ATM fraud? How do these losses compare with the losses due to credit card fraud? Indeed, the two types of analyses -- on the nature and the extent of ATM fraud -- are complementary and both are essential not only to an understanding of ATM fraud but also to a determination of procedures for preventing its incidence.

Before discussing the nature and extent of ATM fraud in Sections 3.2 and 3.3, respectively, we consider some pertinent data collection issues in Section 3.1.

3.1 DATA COLLECTION ISSUES

Inasmuch as this study represents a pilot effort at obtaining ATM fraud data directly from banks, fundamental data collection-related questions need to be addressed. First, do banks maintain records of their ATM incidents? If not, then a retrospective data collection effort would not be possible and incident records must be collected on an on-going or prospective basis. Fortunately, due in part to Reg E, banks do routinely track and maintain documentation of ATM incidents -- at least for those incidents covered by Reg E (i.e., incidents involving accountholder complaints). Consequently, a retrospective approach to collecting ATM-related data has been viable.

Other important considerations include identifying the incident data repositories at the banks. Are there one or several repositories? Are records of ATM incidents kept separate from records of other types of EFT and non-EFT retail banking incidents? Another issue is the form in which the incident information is kept. Are the incident records sufficiently detailed? For example, if banks only record the case number and the financial disposition of each incident, then sufficient information clearly is not available to assess the nature of ATM fraud. At the same time, there are analogous questions regarding the availability and consistency of summary data concerning ATM frauds and losses. For example, are all ATM fraud losses charged to the same account? Are they pooled with non-fraud losses? Are ATM fraud losses of less than, say $100, merged with the "miscellaneous" losses? These and other data collection issues and procedures are considered below, first as they relate to data collection at the incident level, and then as they relate to data collection at the summary level.

Incident Data Collection

In this subsection on data collection at the incident level, we first consider some background issues, and then discuss the pertinent data collection instrument we developed, followed by some remarks on the data samples we obtained.

Background

Collecting ATM incidents from the Panel banks has been contingent on first identifying where the records are kept. Incident data collection would be simple if each bank has a "single file cabinet" devoted exclusively to storing all ATM incidents. Panel banks maintaining incidents in this manner typically have one person or a group of persons within the same department charged with investigating and resolving all ATM incidents. However, at some banks no one department handles all the ATM incidents. In these instances, incidents could be maintained at different locations within a bank based on:

(i)   Type of incident. All incidents might be reported to a central office where they are routed to different departments based on the type of incident. For example, complex incidents involving organized scams require the attention of personnel with special investigative skills, who might be in a different department than personnel who handle the more routine incidents.

(ii) Accountholder's branch. Incidents at some banks are handled at the branch level, where the bank personnel are more familiar with the accountholder. Since bank branches might be located over a large area, such as a statewide or multi-state region, logistical considerations might suggest that a single incident repository would be impractical.

(iii) Both type of incident and accountholder's branch. Under this system, the branches investigate and maintain records of routine incidents involving their accountholders, while deferring more complex and serious incidents to a central or regional investigative office.

Clearly, the three ATM record maintenance systems discussed above require a more complicated data collection effort than if a "single file cabinet" system were used. At Panel banks with multiple data repositories, we did not visit each data repository; instead, we relied on our key ATM contact at the bank to coordinate the data collection.

Although banks have personnel and departments devoted to the investigation and resolution of ATM incidents, sometimes records of ATM incidents, or a certain subset of ATM incidents, are not separated from records of non-ATM incidents, thus further complicating the data collection process. This situation typically arises in smaller banks or banks whose ATM operation is small. As an example,

27

all overdrafts, whether ATM-related or not, could be investigated and maintained by the same department. Further, bad check-related ATM incidents (e.g., stolen or fraudulent checks deposited in an ATM) could be merged with cases involving all bad checks, including those deposited with bank tellers. In other instances, ATM incidents could be pooled with other types of retail EFT incidents, such as POS incidents.

A concurrent concern, along with where incident information is kept, is the form of the information. Specifically, is sufficient information (i.e., sufficient to assess the nature of ATM fraud) maintained about each incident? As mentioned earlier, Reg E ensures that some minimum amount of information would be compiled for each incident that involves an accountholder complaint. In these situations, an incident's "folder" would typically contain four types of information:

(i) Basic accountholder and complaint information. Usually, a formal form is completed with basic accountholder information (e.g., name, address, account number) as well as basic complaint information (e.g., amount of the financial claim, reason for the complaint).

(ii) Transaction information. The number and type of ATM transactions associated with the complaint are contained in the folder; the information might be displayed in summary form or in a transaction log.

(iii) Investigative information. Narrative summaries of interviews with the accountholder and other persons, affidavits, and reports from other investigative units are contained in the incident folder.

(iv) Incident disposition. Finally, the folder contains the bank's decision regarding the disposition of the incident, especially in regard to its financial consequences; the disposition could be in the form of a letter to the accountholder or possibly a bank charge-off slip.

Sometimes, however, especially in smaller banks, reporting procedures are more ad hoc, as no formal ATM incident forms or reporting procedures exist. This might also be true at larger banks in the case of unusual types of ATM incidents, such as those involving employee fraud. Incident records in such cases might be a memorandum written by a bank investigator, or simply handwritten notes attached to a transaction log. (As noted in Section 4.1, the same problems exist in the wire transfer area, where reporting procedures are typically ad hoc because fraudulent wire transfers are rare.)

Despite the above mentioned problems, it was clear from our initial site visits that the Panel banks do have adequate -- Reg E mandated -- data on those ATM incidents involving an accountholder-initiated complaint. On the other hand, documentation of incidents involving only bank-initiated

complaints -- lodged against accountholders, employees or other outsiders -- is typically less complete. Indeed, the lack of formal recordkeeping procedures for these bank-initiated incidents has posed a threat to our collecting a representative sample of all fraud-related ATM incidents -- this is further discussed below as well as in Section 3.2.

Instrument

Developing an ATM incident coding form, one that adequately captures the important information about as many types of incidents as possible, has been an extremely important task. In order for ATM incidents to be detailed on an on-going basis, thereby creating a consolidated and permanent source of information on ATM fraud, an operationally-oriented incident data collection instrument -- and coding form -- had to be developed.

The development process began with our reviewing each Panel bank's incident form to see what type of incident information the banks recorded. It became clear that no one Panel bank's form would be adequate from a coding and analysis perspective, largely because the forms allowed for open-ended narratives. Several drafts of the incident data collection instrument were tested on sample incidents; in fact, it was discovered that only through coding actual incidents could limitations of the instrument be revealed and improvements suggested. In the end, the final draft of the instrument -- as contained in Exhibit A.1 -- represented a synthesis of several incident forms, subject to our need to appropriately code and analyze the data. It should be noted that the instrument is not only adequate for analysis purposes but also for operational use by ATM clerks and investigators. In fact, several questions on the instrument -- most notably the accountholder information -- were included on the form only for operational purposes. Further, the right hand side of the form is blank, allowing room for narrative comments.

The Incident Data Collection Instrument contained in Exhibit A.1 is in five parts. Depending on the type of incident, different parts would be completed. The five parts include:

A. Background. Various accountholder data are required, together with the reason for initiating the complaint. The complaints are separated according to whether they are accountholder-initiated or bank-initiated.

B. Transaction and Disposition. All transactions connected with the incident are described in the transaction history table. The description includes the amount the accountholder states he/she deposited or withdrew; the amount posted by the bank; and whether the transaction is determined by the bank to be authorized or unauthorized. The amount the accountholder and the bank claim is owed to each of them is indicated in the disposition summary table, alongside the initial and final

28

disposition amount. Other questions include reasons for denying a claim; the impact of Reg E on the disposition amounts; and which event occurred between the initial and the final disposition.

C. Deposit-Related Information. If the incident involves a disputed deposit, one of ten causes is selected.

D. Withdrawal-Related Information. If the incident involves a disputed withdrawal, one of eight causes is selected. Then, if the accountholder claims the withdrawal is unauthorized, information on the accountholder's card status is required; if available, the photograph of the person making the transaction is obtained; and if possible, the person making the withdrawal is identified. For those disputed withdrawal incidents in which the card is not in the possession of the accountholder at the time of the disputed withdrawal, several additional questions are required to be answered, including critical dates; how the accountholder lost possession of the card; PIN status; where the card was stolen; what other items were stolen; "hot card" activity; and current status of the card.

E. Reg E Requirements. Upon determination of the critical dates, the bank determines the extent of accountholder liability under Reg E.

Again, it should be noted that while our instrument is more comprehensive than any of the corresponding forms being used by the Panel banks, it would be only partially completed for most incidents, as only a small number of incidents involve both deposit and withdrawal related complications.

Data Samples

The issue of how many ATM incident records should be obtained from each Panel bank had to be determined in the context of our own overall resource constraint and each bank's ability to provide the required records. Obviously, the more incidents we could collect and analyze, the more valid the study results would be from a statistical point of view. However, inasmuch as "processing" an incident (i.e., coding the incident and keying the coded data into a computer database) is quite time consuming, we had to develop a data sampling strategy that could be carried out within our limited resources. Given the needs of our other study activities, we determined that we could afford .to collect, code, key and analyze some 4,000 ATM incident records for the two calendar years of 1983 and 1984. Based on our estimate of the yearly number of incident records compiled by all 16 Study Panel banks, the 4,000 figure implied an approximate 10 percent sample. Indeed, for most of the Panel banks (each with several thousand incident records per year), we requested a 10 percent random sample of their records. (A systematic random

sampling procedure -- that is, every tenth record -- was employed to secure the sample.) For a handful of Panel banks (each with between 50 to 300 incident records per year), we requested a 100 percent sample of their records. This stratified sampling approach compensated for the fact that the Study Panel's composition is somewhat biased towards the large commercial banks which tend to have more extensive EFT experience than the smaller banks. In the end, as detailed in Section 3.2, 2,707 and 1,480 ATM incident records were obtained for the years 1983 and 1984, respectively, for a total of 4,187 records. The key reason the 1983 data sample was larger than the 1984 data sample was because, as noted in Section 2.2, we allowed the Panel banks to provide us with the 1983 data over a 9 month period (i.e., January 1 to September 30, 1984), as compared to a 6 month period (i.e., January 1 to June 30, 1985) for the 1984 data.

Are the obtained data samples representative of the ATM incident experience of the 16 Panel banks? The answer is two-fold. The samples do represent the Panel's experience within each initial complaint category (e.g., unauthorized withdrawals), but they do not represent the Panel's experience when making inter-category comparisons, especially when the comparison is between accountholder-initiated complaints (e.g., unauthorized withdrawals) and bank-initiated complaints (e.g., overdrafts). As noted earlier, the accountholder-initiated complaints are more complete and accessible -- because of Reg E requirements -- than the bank-initiated complaints. Although a fine point is being made here, it is a crucial one and is further discussed in Section 3.2.

Following determination of the incident data samples, the Panel banks were given a choice of either coding the incidents themselves onto our Incident Data Collection Instrument or mailing the incident records to us, with certain confidential data elements -- such as the accountholder's name -- blanked out. Most Panel banks opted for the latter approach and allowed us to code their incidents; in fact, only three banks chose to code their own incidents. Irrespective of the coding approach, we endeavored to maintain a high degree of consistency in interpreting the incident narratives. In this regard, we trained and cross-checked all coders, including those bank personnel who undertook their own coding.

Finally, the coded and completed incident instruments were keyed into a proprietary relational database management system that had been specially modified to reflect the unique characteristics of the ATM Incident Data Collection Instrument. The system contains easy-to-use data entry screens and powerful search and retrieval capabilities that allowed us to perform various in-depth analyses, as detailed in Section 3.2.

Summary Data Collection

An assessment of the nature of ATM fraud could only be obtained by examining individual incidents. Accordingly, as discussed in the previous subsection, we collected ATM incidents from the Panel banks. But what type of data is necessary to assess the extent of ATM fraud (in particular, to estimate the nationwide ATM fraud loss)? Below, we discuss the methods we used to estimate the nationwide ATM fraud loss; the method, in turn, dictated the type of data we needed to collect.

In order to estimate the nationwide ATM fraud loss, it was necessary, first, to determine the total ATM fraud loss at each Panel bank; second, to normalize that figure by an appropriate base; third, to recognize the size of these normalizations -- or loss ratios -- over the various Panel banks; and, fourth, to project or estimate the nationwide fraud loss for a year by multiplying the appropriate loss ratios by the nationwide value of the base for that year. Two pertinent bases were used for our estimates: the number of ATM transactions and the dollar volume of those transactions. (It should be recognized that throughout this report, we use the term ATM "transaction" to refer only to a withdrawal or to a deposit; it does not refer to a balance inquiry, or to a transfer of funds between accounts, or to any other ATM activity.) Although other bases (e.g., number of installed ATMs) could have been used, we felt that they yielded inappropriate or unstable loss ratios. Thus, for example, the loss per installed ATM is quite an unstable ratio, as it is very dependent on where the ATMs are located and how many transactions are processed on them.

In sum, to estimate the nationwide ATM fraud loss by the method described above, the following 1983 and 1984 data had to be collected from each Panel bank: the loss -- actually, net loss -- figure due to fraud, the number of ATM transactions, and the dollar volume of transactions. Additionally, we required nationwide estimates of the total number of transactions and the total dollar volume of transactions for both 1983 and 1984.

Given the above defined needs for summary data, we next consider some background issues, and then discuss the pertinent data collection instrument we developed, followed by some remarks on the data samples we obtained.

Background

As in the case of obtaining a representative sample of ATM incidents, similar problems can occur in trying to obtain accurate summary figures from the banks. Recall that an important factor in the availability of certain ATM incidents concerned who initiated the incident or complaint. When considering the availability of summary data, an analogous situation arises. Here, the primary consideration is to which account are the losses due to fraud charged. Are the losses charged to an account that depends on the type of incident? Does each branch have a ATM fraud loss account? Additional concerns include whether the bank has a separate account for ATM fraud losses or one that is combined with other -- both fraud and non-fraud -- losses.

The presence of ATM networks poses yet another difficulty in collecting consistent summary data; in particular, it tends to blur the distinction between transactions performed on an ATM owned by one bank and transactions performed on an ATM owned by other banks in the network. This difficulty is further complicated when one tries to identify the bank to which the accountholder performing the transaction belongs. All of these complications, in turn, impacts the quality of the available data. As depicted in Exhibit 3.1, a network-based bank only has good fraud-related data on transactions performed on its own ATMs; it has mediocre data, at best, for transactions performed on other network ATMs by its own accountholders. Further, some banks may only know the total number of transactions performed on their own ATMs, without being able to identify the bank affiliation of those making the transactions. On the other hand, a bank that operates the network may have good data for all of the four cells depicted in Exhibit 3.1.

In addition to difficulties in obtaining consistent and valid summary loss and transaction figures, nationwide estimates for the total number of transactions and the corresponding dollar volume are also subject to a certain degree of uncertainty. As indicated in Section 1.1, different industry experts publish different estimates, often provoking a lively debate as to who has the "correct" estimate [Garsson, 1983].

Instrument

For the purpose of collecting summary ATM data from the Panel banks, a Summary Data Collection Instrument was developed; it is contained in Exhibit A.2. The instrument seeks data on the number of installed ATMs, the number of transactions, and the dollar volume of transactions, the number of incidents resulting in dollar loss to the bank, the dollar amount of loss to the bank, and the dollar amount of recovery.

Finally, although not contained in an exhibit in Appendix A, we developed and used another less formal instrument for collecting background information on each Panel bank. The instrument includes such data elements as the bank's card base, PIN characteristics, network affiliation, daily withdrawal limit, etc. This information helped us to understand and interpret our analysis results.

Data Samples

In varying degrees, each Panel bank provided us with some summary and background data. Obviously, as alluded to earlier, the available data were sometimes not detailed enough. For example, one Panel bank only had available the total number of "transactions", which included transfers between accounts and balance inquiries. Nevertheless, as detailed in Section 3.3, we have been able to make estimates of the nationwide ATM fraud loss.

3.2 NATURE OF ATM FRAUD

In this and the next section, we analyze the obtained ATM data separately for the calendar years 1983 and 1984. While the analysis results are presented accordingly, it should be recognized that most of the variations between the two years are not statistically significant -- using a chi-square test at a 0.05 level of significance.

Exhibit 3.1

ATM: Network-Related Data Problems

Transaction Performed By:	Transaction Performed On:	
	Bank A's ATM	Not Bank A's ATM
Bank A's Accountholder	Bank A has good fraud-related data on these transactions.	Bank A has medicore fraud-related data on these transactions.
Not Bank A's Accountholder	Bank A has good fraud-related data on these transactions.	Bank A has no fraud-related data on these transactions.

However, even when the variation is significant, we hesitate to make any strong statements, as more than two years worth of data is needed to establish any meaningful trends. Indeed, in order to obtain larger data samples, it may be more statistically valid to combine the 1983 and 1984 data sets and to present the results in an aggregate manner, as is done in Exhibit A.1 for the ATM incidents.

Our discussion of the nature of ATM fraud is contained in the following eight subsections, each focusing on a different aspect of the fraud problem. The discussion is directed at an ATM incident's initial complaint, amount of claim, complaint cause, potential for fraudulence, lost or stolen card, suspected perpetrator, and financial disposition, followed by some remarks concerning Reg E.

Initial Complaint

The initial complaint which initiates an ATM incident is the logical starting point for any discussion of the nature of ATM fraud. As listed in Exhibit A.1, Question 5, we have identified 11 categories or types of initial complaints; these are described in Exhibit 3.2. The 11 initial complaints are grouped in accordance to whether they are accountholder-initiated or bank-initiated. Such a grouping is not only practically relevant, but also important from a fraud prevention perspective. While the objective is to enhance the ability of both accountholders and bank personnel to initiate a complaint in as timely a manner as possible, the means by which the objective is achieved may be different for accountholders than for bank personnel. For example, an intensive educational program would help accountholders to recognize a potential fraud problem. On the other hand, bank personnel would be helped by sophisticated computer algorithms that could automatically detect any out of the ordinary or suspicious transaction.

It is to be noted that the list of initial complaints in Exhibit 3.2 includes a "other" category. This category could contain any of the potential frauds identified in Exhibit 1.9 but not explicitly listed in Exhibit 3.2, including, as examples, insider manipulations or external attacks on an ATM. It should not be construed that the "other" complaints are not important; rather their omission simply recognizes the apparent rarity of their occurrence or, at least, the rarity of their being formally reported. Another issue of note is that although we assign only one initial complaint type to each incident, multiple-complaint incidents can, and do, occur. For example, consider the following scenario. The bank notices that an account is overdrawn due to an ATM withdrawal. The bank subsequently informs the accountholder of this situation, who immediately realizes that his card is missing and therefore claims that the most recent withdrawals against his account were made by somebody else and therefore not authorized by him. In such multiple-complaint incidents, the "initial" -- in the chronological sense -- complaint is selected. Thus, in the above scenario, an overdraft, and not an unauthorized withdrawal, would be the initial complaint. However, the requirement that only the initial complaint type in a

multiple-complaint incident should be coded should not be viewed as a limitation of our Incident Data Collection Instrument since subsequent questions on the instrument do solicit the additional information. For example, returning to the above scenario, the fact that the accountholder disputed one or more withdrawals would be indicated in Questions 8 and 13 through 25 in Exhibit A.1.

Exhibit 3.3 shows the breakdown of ATM incidents by type of initial complaint. Most of the incidents which the banks provided to us are accountholder-initiated: 89.1 percent of the 2,707 1983 incidents and 94.9 percent of the 1,480 1984 incidents are accountholder-initiated. The low number of bank-initiated complaints can, as noted in Section 3.1, be partially explained by the fact that since Reg E does not apply to incidents which do not involve an accountholder claim, these complaints are not well documented and/or reported. Indeed, Exhibit 3.3 shows that only a handful of the Panel banks reported bank-initiated complaints. (The decrease in the number of Panel banks reporting data in 1984, as compared to 1983, can, as pointed out in Section 3.1, be explained by the shorter period in 1984, as compared to 1983, during which we allowed the Panel banks to provide us with data.) In addition to Reg E, several other reasons prevented one or more Panel banks from providing us with certain incident data, including resource and time constraints, logistical problems due to multiple data repositories, poor recordkeeping, and no experience with specific types of complaints. Consequently, if the latter reason were to be taken into consideration, the number of Panel banks providing us with data by each type of initial complaint would be at least as many as the corresponding number of Panel banks reporting -- see Exhibit 3.3 -- such a complaint, since although a bank might want to provide us with the data, it could not report any as it had no such experience.

What are the implications of the above identified reporting difficulties? Several comments can be made. First, as discussed in Section 3.1, the key -- and only -- implication is that the obtained incident samples are representative of the experience of the 16 Panel banks on one level but not on another. More specifically, because bank-to-bank comparisons of the nature of the incidents within an initial complaint category are quite consistent, it can be stated that all conditional (i.e., conditional on an initial complaint category) sets of incidents are representative and therefore valid conclusions can be drawn concerning each category, provided, of course, that the size of the data sample in the category is large enough. Thus, referring to Exhibit 3.3, the 1,189 unauthorized withdrawal incidents in 1983 do reflect the unauthorized withdrawal problem of the Panel banks; similarly, the 194 overdraft incidents in 1983 do reflect the overdraft problem of the Panel banks. On the other hand, the reporting difficulties render any inter-category analysis invalid. Thus, the column percentage figures in Exhibit 3.3 are not indicative of the true distribution of ATM incidents by type of initial complaint; as examples, unauthorized withdrawals were probably not 43.9 percent of the total incidents in 1983, nor were overdrafts 7.2

Exhibit 3.2

ATM: Types of Initial Complaints

INITIAL COMPLAINT	DESCRIPTION
Accountholder-Initiated:	
Unauthorized Withdrawals	Accountholder claims he/she did not authorize one or more ATM withdrawals that were debited to his/her account.
Short (Due to Dispensing)	Accountholder claims a discrepancy exists between the amount requested from and the amount dispensed by the ATM.
Deposit Not Credited	Accountholder claims he/she was not credited for a deposit made at the ATM.
Short (Due to Posting)	Accountholder claims a discrepancy exists between the amount dispensed by the ATM and the amount posted to his/her account.
Deposit Credited, But Erroneously	Accountholder claims an ATM desposit was credited, but for an incorrect amount.
Other	Accountholder makes an ATM-related claim other than those listed above.
Bank-Initiated:	
Overdraft	Bank claims on overdraft occurred as a result of an ATM withdrawal.
Stolen/Fraudulent Check Deposited	Bank claims a stolen or fraudulent check was deposited in the ATM.
Empty Envelope Deposited	Bank claims no funds were placed in the deposit envelope, although the cardholder indicated a deposit was made at the ATM.
Uncollectible Check Deposited	Bank claims an uncollectible (other than stolen or fraudulent) check was deposited at the ATM.
Other	Bank makes an ATM-related claim other than those listed above.

Exhibit 3.3

ATM: Incidents By Type Of Initial Complaint

Initial Complaint	ATM Incidents (1983/1984)		Number of Panel Banks Reporting Complaint (1983/1984)
	Number	Column %	
Accountholder-Initiated:			
1. Unauthorized Withdrawals	1189/ 618	43.9%/41.8%	13/8
2. Short (Due to Dispensing)	603/ 487	22.3 /32.9	11/8
3. Deposit Not Credited	441/ 162	16.3 /10.9	9/6
4. Short (Due to Posting)	81/ 79	3.0 / 5.3	11/7
5. Deposit Credited, But Erroneously	63/ 54	2.3 / 3.7	9/5
6. Other	36/ 4	1.3 / 0.3	8/1
Subtotal	2413/1404	89.1 /94.9	--/ --
Bank-Initiated:			
7. Overdraft	194/ 57	7.2 / 3.9	6/6
8. Stolen/Fraudulent Check Deposited	47/ 2	1.7 / 0.1	2/1
9. Empty Envelope Deposited	31/ 6	1.1 / 0.4	3/4
10. Uncollectible (Other Than Stolen/ Fradudulent) Check Deposited	15/ 8	0.6 / 0.5	2/1
11. Other	5/ 3	0.2 / 0.2	3/2
Subtotal	292/ 76	10.8 / 5.1	--/ --
12. Unreported	2/ 0	0.1 / --	2/ --
TOTAL	2707/1480	100.0%/100.0%	--/ --

34

percent of the total incidents in 1983. Could valid inter-category analysis be undertaken? The answer is yes -- by analyzing a subset of the data, the subset belonging to those banks which provide data for all the categories. (When we analyzed such a subset for our Panel banks, we found that unauthorized withdrawals accounted for slightly less than 40 percent of the total incidents in 1983, and overdrafts accounted for slightly more than 10 percent of the total incidents in 1983.) We do not, however, present our subset data analysis in this report, as the appropriate subset of data is indeed a small data sample and subject to the corresponding problems of statistical validity.

The second comment that should be made is that the aforementioned reporting difficulties concerning ATM incidents has had no impact on our analysis of the extent of the ATM fraud problem. As detailed in Section 3.3, our extent analysis is based on summary loss figures maintained by the Panel banks, not on the individual incident data.

Finally, it should be stated that the reporting difficulties have not compromised the purpose of this pilot effort; indeed, the 4,187 incidents obtained from the Panel banks clearly suggest that banks are willing to provide pertinent and consistent ATM fraud data. Further, this sample represents by far the largest set of ATM incidents ever collected and analyzed.

Amount of Claim

In each ATM incident, there is, of course, a dispute: the accountholder could claim he/she is owed money (e.g., in the case of unauthorized withdrawals); the bank could claim it is owed money (e.g., in the case of an overdraft); or both the accountholder and the bank could claim that they are each owed money (e.g., in the case of an overdraft which the accountholder claims is due to an unauthorized withdrawal). As an example of the latter type of dispute, consider the following incident that occurred at a Midwestern Panel bank in 1984. An accountholder with $200 in his account had his card stolen. The person now possessing the card deposited $1,000 worth of stolen checks at an ATM, thus inflating the account balance to $1,200. Subsequently, the person withdrew all $1,200 from the account. In this instance, the accountholder claimed that he was owed $200, while the bank claimed that it was owed $1,000.

Exhibit 3.4 summarizes the amount claimed for each of the incidents by type of initial complaint. As expected, the majority of accountholder-initiated incidents involves only an accountholder claim: in 1983, for example, the 2,343 reported accountholder-initiated claims resulted in only 58 reported bank counter-claims. Similarly, bank-initiated incidents involve few accountholder counter-claims. Regarding the actual dollar amounts, it is interesting to note that in the category with the largest sample size -- the unauthorized withdrawal category --the dollar amount of the claim did not change significantly from 1983 ($287) to 1984 ($301). Likewise, the amount claimed on shorts due to dispensing remained stable ($48 in 1983 and

$46 in 1984). While the small sample sizes must be taken into consideration, it should be noted that bank-initiated incidents typically involve higher dollar claims. As an example, the 33 bank claims in stolen/fraudulent check deposit incidents in 1983 averaged $1,032.

How are these claims disposed of? As discussed in the following subsections, some claims are withdrawn for a variety of reasons, while others are settled subject to the requirements of Reg E.

Complaint Cause

As listed in the Incident Data Collection Instrument (Exhibit A.1, Questions 12 and 13), we identified 10 deposit-related causes and 8 withdrawal-related causes. These causes were, again, chosen on the likelihood of their occurrence. Each incident involving at least one withdrawal was assigned one, and only one, withdrawal-related cause; similarly, each incident involving at least one deposit was assigned one, and only one, deposit-related cause. Just as an incident could involve multiple complaints, an incident could be attributable to multiple withdrawal-related causes and/or multiple deposit-related causes. For example, an overdraft might have been caused by the bank's computer being off-line; yet, the overdraft would not have occurred if the accountholder's card had not been stolen. In a withdrawal or deposit case involving multiple causes, we selected the primary, or most important, cause. In a case involving both withdrawals and deposits, as well as multiple causes, we selected both a withdrawal-related cause and a deposit-related cause. It is for this reason that, as shown in Exhibit 3.5, the total number of causes is greater than the total number of complaints or incidents: the 2,707 1983 incidents and the 1,480 1984 incidents were due to 2,817 and 1,534 causes, respectively. (The row percentages in the exhibit are based on the total number of causes, not the total number of distinct incidents.) Before discussing in the following subsections the causes by type of complaint, one should note the large number of zero percentages in the exhibit, indicating that most of the incidents are due to only two or three main causes.

Causes of Unauthorized Withdrawals

The leading cause of unauthorized withdrawal incidents is lost or stolen ATM cards, accounting for 47.4 percent (45.3 percent) of that type of incident in 1983 (1984). Due to the importance of this cause of ATM fraud, several questions on the Incident Data Collection Instrument specifically address the issue of lost or stolen cards, and a later subsection is devoted to this issue. Meanwhile, it should be noted that the distribution of unauthorized withdrawal causes is comparable for the two years; this supports our earlier statement regarding the comparability of the results for the two years. Additionally, because of the comparability finding and the fact that half as many unauthorized withdrawal incidents were provided by the Panel banks in 1984 as in 1983, the Exhibit 3.5 results for unauthorized withdrawals also support our claim that the data sample for each initial complaint category -- in this case, unauthorized

Exhibit 3.4

ATM: Incidents By Amount Of Claim

Initial Complaint	Total Number of Incidents (1983/1984)	Incidents Reporting A Claim (1983/1984)			
		Accountholder Claim		Bank Claim	
		Number	$ Average	Number	$ Average
Accountholder-Initiated:					
1. Unauthorized Withdrawal	1189/618	1151/559	$287/$301	46/19	$283/$507
2. Short (Due to Dispensing)	603/487	594/478	$48/$46	7/9	$21/$50
3. Deposit Not Credited	441/162	434/162	$448/$350	0/0	--/--
4. Short (Due to Posting)	81/79	76/70	$78/$64	2/9	$35/$127
5. Deposit Credited, But Erroneously	63/54	61/48	$370/$152	1/5	$1/$196
6. Other	36/4	27/4	$322/$95	2/0	$58/--
SUBTOTAL	2413/1404	2343/1321	$252/$196	58/42	$230/$291
Bank-Initiated:					
7. Overdraft	194/57	12/1	$777/$1	185/52	$228/$286
8. Stolen/Fraudulent Check Deposited	47/2	5/0	$292/--	33/0	$1032/--
9. Empty Envelope Desposited	31/6	8/1	$228/$50	19/3	$269/$828
10. Uncollectible (Other Than Stolen/Fraudulent) Check Deposited	15/8	1/0	$200/--	13/8	$705/$205
11. Other	5/3	2/0	$100/--	3/2	$39/$3931
SUBTOTAL	292/76	28/2	$465/$26	253/65	$358/$413
12. Unreported	2/0	1/--	$960/--	1/--	$15/--
TOTAL	2707/1480	2372/1323	$255/$196	312/107	$333/$365

Exhibit 3.5

ATM: Initial Complaint By Cause

Cause of Initial Complaint by Row Percent (1983/1984)

Initial Complaint	Total Number of Distinct Incidents (1983/1984)	Total Number of Causes (1983/1984)	Withdrawal Related Cause								Deposit-Related Cause											19. Disregarded
			1. A/H Had Card Lost/Stolen	2. A/H Had Card in Possession But Transaction Unauthorized	3. A/H Withdrew Against Bad Deposit	4. A/H Confused	5. Bank's Computer Off-Line	6. Bank's Delayed Posting Procedure	7. Bank's ATM Had Mechanical Problem	8. Other	9. A/H Deposited Empty Envelope	10. A/H Deposited in Wrong Account	11. A/H Indicated Wrong Deposit Account	12. A/H Deposited Stolen/Fraudulent Check	13. A/H Deposited Uncollectible Check	14. A/H Confused	15. A/H Posted Incorrect Amount	16. Bank Posted To Wrong Account	17. Person Other Than A/H Made Bad Deposit	18. Other		
Accountholder-Initiated:																						
1. Unauthorized Withdrawal	1185/ 610	1220/ 640	47.4%/45.3%	25.2/25.5	0.5/ 0.1	12.5/16.4	1.5/0.1	0.2/0.1	0.7/ 1.0	4.4/ 1.2	0.2/ 0.0	0.0/ 0.0	0.0/ 0.0	0.0/ 0.2	0.0/0.0	0.0/ 0.0	0.0/ 0.0	0.0/0.0	1.6/ 5.5	0.1/ 0.2	5.7/ 3.6
2. Short (Dispensing)	603/ 607	603/ 607	0.0%/ 0.0%	0.2/ 0.0	0.0/ 0.0	11.0/12.1	0.0/0.0	0.2/0.0	84.0/83.0	0.0/ 1.0	0.0/ 0.0	0.0/ 0.0	0.0/ 0.0	0.0/ 0.0	0.0/0.0	0.0/ 0.0	0.0/ 0.0	0.0/0.0	0.0/ 0.0	0.0/ 0.0	3.8/ 3.1
3. Deposit Not Credited	441/ 162	442/ 162	0.0%/ 0.0%	0.0/ 0.0	0.0/ 0.0	0.0/ 0.0	0.0/0.0	0.0/0.0	0.2/ 0.0	0.0/ 0.0	2.5/ 4.3	11.1/21.0	2.3/ 3.7	0.0/ 0.0	2.3/1.2	28.7/14.2	6.1/24.7	5.0/4.9	0.2/ 0.0	7.0/18.5	34.6/ 7.5
4. Short (Posting)	81/ 79	81/ 81	0.0%/ 0.0%	2.5/ 0.0	0.0/ 0.0	19.7/32.1	0.0/1.0	0.0/0.0	74.1/65.5	1.2/ 0.0	0.0/ 0.0	0.0/ 0.0	0.0/ 0.0	0.0/ 0.0	0.0/0.0	0.0/ 0.0	0.0/ 1.2	0.0/0.0	0.0/ 0.0	0.0/ 1.2	2.5/ 0.0
5. Deposit Credited Erroneously	63/ 54	63/ 54	0.0%/ 0.0%	0.0/ 0.0	0.0/ 0.0	0.0/ 0.0	0.0/0.0	0.0/0.0	0.0/ 0.0	0.0/ 0.0	0.0/ 0.0	1.6/ 1.9	50.8/59.0	0.0/ 0.0	1.6/0.0	15.9/14.8	22.2/25.9	1.6/1.8	0.0/ 0.0	0.0/ 0.0	6.3/ 3.6
6. Other	36/ 4	16/ 4	37.5%/ 0.0%	0.0/ 0.0	6.2/ 0.0	0.0/ 0.0	6.2/0.0	18.7/0.0	0.0/ 0.0	6.2/100.0	0.0/ 0.0	0.0/ 0.0	0.0/ 0.0	0.0/ 0.0	0.0/0.0	0.0/ 0.0	0.0/ 0.0	6.3/0.0	0.0/ 0.0	6.3/ 0.0	6.3/ 0.0
Subtotal	2413/1484	2425/1447	24.1%/20.6%	12.0/11.6	0.3/ 0.1	9.7/13.3	0.6/0.1	0.3/0.1	23.7/32.4	2.5/ 1.4	0.5/ 0.5	2.1/ 2.4	1.7/ 2.3	0.0/ 0.1	0.5/0.1	5.6/ 2.1	1.7/ 3.0	1.0/1.6	0.9/ 2.5	1.4/ 2.2	10.4/ 3.0
Bank-Initiated:																						
7. Overdraft	19%/ 57	20%/ 62	0.2%/ 1.6	0.5/ 1.6	6.3/12.9	0.0/ 0.0	71.6/19.4	1.9/37.2	1.0/0.0	1.0/ 0.0	3.4/ 0.0	0.0/ 0.0	0.0/ 0.0	0.0/ 1.6	1.0/0.0	0.0/ 0.0	0.5/ 3.2	0.0/0.0	2.3/ 1.6	0.0/ 0.0	2.3/14.5
8. Stolen/Fraudulent Check Deposited	47/ 2	9%/ 4	29.0%/25.0%	0.0/ 0.0	14.0/25.0	0.0/ 0.0	0.0/ 0.0	0.0/0.0	0.0/0.0	1.1/ 0.0	1.1/ 0.0	0.0/ 0.0	0.0/ 0.0	10.9/25.0	0.0/0.0	0.0/ 0.0	0.0/ 0.0	0.0/0.0	33.3/25.0	0.0/ 0.0	10.7/ 0.0
9. Empty Envelope Deposited	31/ 6	56/ 11	23.2%/ 0.0%	1.8/ 0.0	12.5/27.3	0.0/ 0.0	1.8/ 0.0	0.0/0.0	0.0/0.0	0.0/ 9.1	14.3/45.4	0.0/ 0.0	0.0/ 0.0	0.0/ 0.0	0.0/0.0	0.0/ 0.0	0.0/ 0.0	0.0/0.0	12.1/ 9.1	3.6/ 0.0	10.7/ 9.1
10. Uncollectible Check Deposited	15/ 8	28/ 8	0.0%/ 0.0%	0.0/ 0.0	39.2/ 0.0	0.0/12.5	0.0/0.0	0.0/0.0	0.0/ 0.0	7.1/ 0.0	0.0/ 0.0	0.0/ 0.0	0.0/ 0.0	0.0/ 0.0	42.9/87.5	0.0/ 0.0	0.0/ 0.0	0.0/0.0	3.6/ 0.0	3.6/ 0.0	3.6/ 0.0
11. Other	5/ 3	5/ 2	40.0%/ 0.0%	0.0/ 0.0	0.0/ 0.0	0.0/ 0.0	0.0/0.0	0.0/0.0	20.0/0.0	0.0/ 0.0	0.0/ 0.0	0.0/ 0.0	20.0/ 0.0	0.0/ 0.0	0.0/50.0	0.0/ 0.0	0.0/50.0	0.0/0.0	0.0/ 0.0	0.0/ 0.0	20.0/ 0.0
Subtotal	292/ 76	390/ 87	15.1%/ 5.7%	0.5/ 1.1	11.3/13.8	0.0/ 1.2	0.0/23.5	1.0/0.0	0.3/0.0	1.4/ 1.2	4.1/ 6.9	0.0/ 0.0	0.3/ 0.0	2.6/ 2.3	3.6/ 9.2	0.0/ 3.4	0.3/ 3.4	0.0/0.0	14.0/ 3.4	0.0/ 0.0	5.0/13.5
12. Unreported	2/ 0	2/ 0	0.0%/ —	0.0/ —	0.0/ —	0.0/ —	50.0/—	0.0/—	0.0/ —	0.0/ —	0.0/ —	0.0/ —	0.0/ —	0.0/ —	0.0/ —	0.0/ —	0.0/ —	0.0/—	0.0/ —	0.0/ —	50.0/ —
TOTAL	2707/1640	2817/1514	22.5%/19.0%	11.1/11.0	1.8/ 0.9	8.1/12.6	6.1/0.9	0.3/1.6	20.6/30.6	2.3/1.4	1.0/0.9	1.0/2.3	1.5/ 2.1	0.3/ 0.2	0.9/ 0.6	4.9/ 2.0	1.5/ 3.7	0.9/0.6	2.7/ 2.5	1.3/2.1	9.8/ 4.2

*Each incident can have one or more causes.

withdrawals -- is representative of the Panel banks' aggregate experience.

Given that in slightly more than half of the unauthorized withdrawal incidents the accountholder does have his/her card in possession, the question arises as to what are the possible causes of the unauthorized withdrawal incidents when the card is in the accountholder's possession? Four causes are common:

(i) Someone fraudulently uses the card and then replaces it without the accountholder knowing it was ever missing. For example, at a bank in the Northeast, an accountholder recently claimed she did not make two $100 withdrawals that appeared on her monthly statement. She informed the bank that she thought her card had always been in her possession. Photographs taken during the transactions showed that the accountholder's ex-husband made the withdrawals. The accountholder then realized that her ex-husband must have taken, used, and returned her card without her knowledge. Another example involved an apartment building manager who entered a tenant's apartment in the morning, used the card during the day, and then returned it before the tenant returned from work.

(ii) The accountholder actually makes the withdrawals, but does not recall making them. In other words, the accountholder is confused. If the accountholder realizes this, then he/she would typically withdraw the complaint.

(iii) The accountholder actually makes the withdrawals and is trying to defraud the bank. In such instances, the accountholder would adamantly insist that he/she did not make the transactions, possibly threatening legal action if the claim is denied. While it seems odd that an accountholder trying to defraud a bank would claim his/her card is in his/her possession, this scenario does occur, and it is often difficult to prove that the accountholder is trying to defraud the bank. In one incident, however, the bank investigator listened patiently to the accountholder's claim, and then said, in an attempt to bluff the accountholder, "Let me have the pictures taken by the camera of the person making the transactions delivered here so that we can both look at them." At that point, the accountholder suddenly "remembered" that he in fact had made the transactions.

(iv) An ATM system malfunction occurs and the accountholder's card had actually not been used to make the withdrawal. Occasionally, a system failure could cause one account to be "crossed" with another, so that one accountholder's card is

incorrectly allowed to withdraw funds from another accountholder's account.

Unfortunately, it is usually difficult to place an unauthorized withdrawal incident in which the accountholder is still in possession of his/her card in one of the above four categories, due in part to the bank's inability to identify the person or perpetrator making the withdrawal. Although a following subsection considers the identity of the suspected perpetrator, it should be noted that to most of the Panel banks, the identity of the perpetrator is not of critical importance in these "card in possession" incidents, as the banks automatically deny the accountholder's claim in such instances -- reasoning that if the card were in the accountholder's possession, then the transaction must have been authorized. Interestingly, at least one Panel bank typically takes the opposite action; it honors the claim in such instances, because its legal counsel has concluded that it must do so in order to comply with Reg E.

Causes of Shorts

Shorts are far less complicated than unauthorized withdrawal incidents for the simple reason that there is no uncertainty regarding who made the transaction: the accountholder acknowledges making the transaction and only disputes the manner in which it was processed. Exhibit 3.5 shows that a clear majority of the shorts are caused by mechanical problems, indicating that the accountholder who claims money was not dispensed -- or did not get posted -- properly is most likely correct in his/her assertion. In 1983, 84.0 percent of the shorts due to dispensing and 74.1 percent of the shorts due to posting were due to mechanical problems. These percentages remained fairly constant in 1984. Accountholder confusion was the only other frequent cause.

Causes of Deposits Not Credited Properly

While, again, less complex than unauthorized withdrawals, deposit not credited -- or credited erroneously -- incidents are a leading reason for "ATM phobia": acountholders are wary of entrusting a monthly paycheck to a "machine" for processing. There are three typical causes of such incidents.

(i) Bank makes an error in either posting the wrong amount or crediting the wrong account; it could be due to a computer-related failure or to a clerical error. Exhibit 3.5 shows that a significant percentage of these accountholder-initiated incidents is due to such a bank error.

(ii) The accountholder makes an error in the deposit, including forgetting to place the check or cash in the deposit envelope (i.e., depositing an "empty" envelope); depositing an uncollectible check; indicating the wrong dollar amount on the envelope and /or keying the wrong deposit amount into the ATM; or depositing in the wrong account (e.g.,

38

depositing into the savings instead of the checking account). Indeed, for the "deposit credited erroneously" incidents, the leading cause is accountholder errors due to indicating the wrong deposit amount (50.8 percent of the 63 1983 incidents and 50.0 percent of the 54 1984 incidents).

(iii) The bank finds no evidence of a deposit or that the deposit was indeed processed properly. We labelled such incidents as "accountholder confused", recognizing, of course, the possibility that the accountholder might have been trying to defraud the bank.

Causes of Overdraft

Overdrafts due to ATM withdrawals are the most common type of bank-initiated complaint in the sample, accounting for 66.4 percent of the 292 1983 bank-initiated incidents and 75.0 percent of the 76 1984 bank-initiated incidents. How is it that ATM users are able to overdraw accounts? The overdraft incidents in the sample reflect three main causes: (i) the bank's computer being "off-line"; (ii) the bank's delayed posting procedure; and (iii) withdrawals being made against bad deposits. Each of these is discussed below.

A bank's computer is "off-line" when either the computer is inoperable or the communication links between the computer and its ATMs are inoperable. If an off-line situation exists, then the accountholder's account balance -- that is being maintained in the computer -- cannot be accessed by an ATM. Of course, computers are generally on-line and will only go "off-line" in case of a system failure or for system maintenance. When a bank's computer is off-line, the bank generally has backup controls that can be activated. For example, a "hot card" list (i.e., a list of cards that have expired or have been reported missing) may be temporarily "downloaded" to each ATM (i.e., stored in the ATM's memory device). On the other hand, some banks do not allow their ATMs to operate at all in an off-line mode.

Delayed posting procedure is the second main cause of ATM overdrafts. Because of the delayed posting procedure, the ATM would only have access to account balances that might be up to 24 hours out-of-date. Consequently, an overdraft could occur if two or more withdrawals -- amounting to a sum that exceeds the actual account balance -- are made within a short time period. Obviously, an incident of this type does not occur for those banks which have an immmediate posting procedure.

Finally, the third major cause of overdrafts is withdrawals made against bad deposits. Such deposits can be used to "inflate" an account, and any withdrawals made against these deposits that altogether would exceed the accountholder's actual balance would result in an overdraft. A more detailed discussion of this cause of overdrafts is

provided in the next subsection on the causes of bank-initiated deposit-related incidents.

Two points should be made concerning the fact that the distribution of causes of overdraft for 1983 is significantly different than that for 1984. First, although Exhibit 3.3 states that six banks provided overdraft data for each of the two years, they were not the same six banks, so that some of the causal differences can be attributed to differences between the two groups of banks. For example, we know that the 1984 group of six banks included fewer banks that allowed off-line ATM operation than the 1983 group of six banks; thus, it is not surprising to see in Exhibit 3.5 that only 19.4 percent of the overdrafts in 1984 were caused by the bank's computer being off-line, as compared to 71.6 percent in 1983. A second, and perhaps more important, reason for the causal differences is the small number of overdrafts obtained in 1984; certainly, 57 overdraft incidents do no constitute an adequate sample for extensive analysis.

Causes of Bank-Initiated Deposit-Related Incidents

The problem of small sample sizes is also the reason why the bank-initiated deposit-related incidents -- including stolen/fraudulent checks deposited, empty envelopes deposited, and uncollectible (other than stolen or fraudulent) checks deposited -- cannot be extensively analyzed. Nevertheless, it can be stated that both lost or stolen cards and accountholder misconduct can result in this type of incidents. It can also be stated that deposit-related incidents are generally quite serious in terms of financial consequences. For example, an accountholder at a Northeast bank deposited checks totalling $3,000 in various ATMs. Later, the accountholder began withdrawing on these deposits, which had not yet "cleared" but for which the bank had granted provisional credit. By the time the bank discovered the checks were stolen, the accountholder had drawn -- actually overdrawn --$2,300 from his account. The bank was never able to locate the accountholder. As another example, an accountholder at a Midwestern bank had his card and PIN stolen. He didn't realize this had happened for a week. During that week, the thief and his accomplices, who operated an ATM scam operation, deposited a series of fraudulent checks in various ATMs and made withdrawals against those deposits. In the end, the bank sustained a $2,000 loss.

Other Causes

As indicated in Exhibit 3.5, less than 4 percent of the total causes are contained in the two "other" cause categories, suggesting that the 16 specified causes are able to explain for the various ATM incidents. It should be stated that none of the "other" causes involved electronic attacks on data communication lines; manipulation of ATM software, account information, or transaction data; or other acts requiring special knowledge of computers or communications technology. Additionally, as with most causes, the "other" causes may or may not lead to a fraudulent incident. In the next subsection, we distinguish between incidents that are potentially fraudulent and those that are not.

Potential for Fraud

Just as a small fraction of all ATM transactions are involved in ATM incidents, only a proportion of ATM incidents involve fraudulent activity. Because the focus of this study is on EFT fraud, it is necessary to distinguish between those incidents that involve fraud and those that do not. In many cases, the distinction is not clear. For example, in one incident involving a Panel bank from the Northeast, an accountholder complained that someone used his ATM card to make unauthorized withdrawals totaling $600. But since the accountholder had possession of his card and claimed that he had never lost possession of it, the bank ruled that the withdrawals were "authorized" and that therefore the accountholder was not entitled to a reimbursement. It is unclear whether the man was simply confused and had actually made the withdrawals (i.e., no fraud was involved); or the man actually made the withdrawals and was trying to defraud the bank; or someone else had actually used his card fraudulently.

The object, nevertheless, is to identify a consistent sample of "potentially fraudulent" ATM incidents, culled from all the ATM incidents provided by the Panel banks. We refer to the incidents as "potentially fraudulent" -- as opposed to "fraudulent" -- because in nearly all cases, no legal action has been taken against the suspected perpetrator. (Indeed, legal action was initiated by the bank in only a handful of the 4,187 ATM incidents that we analyzed; these were mostly situations involving an organized scam.) These potentially fraudulent incidents provided an appropriate basis for our analysis of ATM fraud. Moreover, such a sample of incidents overcame some of the data-related inconsistencies among our Panel banks; irrespective of what records are kept by each bank and what records were provided to us, we were able to abstract a consistent set of potentially fraudulent incidents for analysis.

For the purpose of this effort, an incident was labeled "potentially fraudulent" primarily because of its associated cause(s). Based on the 19 causes identified in Exhibit 3.5, Exhibit 3.6 shows how a cause is determined to be potentially fraudulent. Seven causes are automatically defined as potentially fraudulent. Most conspicuous in this group of causes are the lost and stolen card incidents. The other causes include: the accountholder having the card in possession but still claiming that unauthorized transactions have been made; overdrafts caused by an accountholder withdrawing against a bad or insufficient deposit; overdrafts caused by a bank's computer being off-line; overdrafts caused by a bank's delayed posting procedure; an accountholder depositing a stolen/fraudulent check; and a person other than the accountholder making a bad deposit. Incidents involving five other causes are potentially fraudulent only if the bank has sustained a loss: they include "other" withdrawal-related causes; an accountholder depositing an empty envelope; an accountholder depositing an uncollectible (but not stolen/fraudulent)

check; "other" deposit-related causes; and "unreported" causes. Using bank loss as the criterion for determining if an incident is potentially fraudulent is appropriate, as any loss sustained by a bank is not only documentable but also probably implies that someone -- the accountholder, another person, or a bank employee -- received an undeserved (i.e., in a potentially fraudulent manner) amount of money equal to the bank loss. Another possible determination criterion could be accountholder loss beyond the Reg E stipulated amount; such a criterion would, however, be difficult to effect in practice, as it is almost impossible to establish with certainty the validity of an accountholder's claim. Finally, incidents involving the remaining seven causes (i.e., accountholder confusion on a withdrawal-related incident; bank's ATM having a mechanical problem; accountholder depositing a check in the wrong account; accountholder depositing an amount different than that indicated on the envelope and/or that keyed into the ATM; accountholder confusion on a deposit-related incident; bank posting the wrong amount; and bank posting the deposit to a wrong account) are automatically defined as being not potentially fraudulent. It should be noted that the determinations in Exhibit 3.6 are conservative, for the most part, even though they are not based on formal legal proceedings. Thus, certain incidents which might indeed result in an accountholder loss beyond the Reg E stipulated amount may not be categorized as being potentially fraudulent, nor may certain incidents which might indeed be attempted, but unsuccessful frauds (e.g., an accountholder feigning confusion after being discovered).

The results of applying the Exhibit 3.6 determinations to the Exhibit 3.5 causes are contained in Exhibit 3.7. In accordance with the determinations, most incidents are designated on the basis of their cause(s) as being either potentially fraudulent or not, while some of them are designated on the basis of whether a bank loss occurred -- for example, 58.6 percent or 17 of the 29 1983 empty envelope incidents resulted in a bank loss and are therefore categorized as being potentially fraudulent. In total, 47.5 percent of the total number of causes in 1983 are categorized as being potentially fraudulent; the corresponding figure in 1984 is 37.6 percent. This decrease merely reflects the fact that relatively more potentially fraudulent incidents were provided by the Panel banks in 1983 than in 1984. Because each ATM incident can have one or more causes, Exhibit 3.7 indicates that the total number of causes is slightly larger that the total number of distinct incidents; additionally, the proportion categorized as potentially fraudulent is slightly larger when considering the causes than when considering the incidents.

Actually, the breakdown of incidents by type of initial complaint and potential to be fraudulent is given in Exhibit 3.8. It is seen that the vast majority of the potentially fraudulent incidents are unauthorized withdrawals: 921 of the 1,189 (i.e., 77.5 percent) and 472 of the 618 (i.e., 76.4 percent) unauthorized withdrawals were determined to be potentially fraudulent in 1983 and 1984, respectively. The fact that

Exhibit 3.6

ATM: Determining Potentially Fraudulent Incidents

Cause of Complaint	Determination		
	Always Potentially Fraudulent	Potentially Fraudulent Only If Bank Sustains Loss	Not Potentially Fraudulent
Withdrawal-Related:			
1. Accountholder (A/H) Had Card Lost/Stolen (Causing Unauthorized Transaction)	X		
2. A/H Had Card In Possession But Transaction Unauthorized	X		
3. A/H Withdrew Against Insufficient/Bad Deposit (Causing Overdraft)	X		
4. A/H Confused — No Error			X
5. Bank's Computer Was Off-Line (Causing Overdraft)	X		
6. Bank's Delayed Posting Procedure (Causing Overdraft)	X		
7. Bank's ATM Had Mechanical Problem (Causing Short/ Over or Wrong Posting)			X
8. Other		X	
Deposit-Related:			
9. A/H Deposited Empty Envelope		X	
10. A/H Deposited In Wrong Account			X
11. A/H Deposited Amount Different Than That Indicated On Envelope And/Or That Keyed Into ATM			X
12. A/H Deposited Stolen/Fraudulent Check	X		
13. A/H Deposited Uncollectible (Other Than Stolen/ Fraudulent) Check		X	
14. A/H Confused — No Error			X
15. Bank Posted Incorrect Amount			X
16. Bank Posted To Wrong Account			X
17. Person Other Than A/H Made Bad Deposit	X		
18. Other		X	
19. Unreported		X	

Exhibit 3.7

ATM: Incidents by Cause of Complaint and Potential to be Fraudulent

Cause of Complaint	Number of ATM Incidents Involved (1983/1984)			
	Total Sample		Potentially Fraudulent	
	Number	Column %	Number	Row %
Withdrawal-Related:				
1. Accountholder (A/H) Had Card Lost/Stolen (Causing Unauthorized Transaction)	644/ 304	22.9%/ 19.8%	644/ 304	100.0%/100.0%
2. A/H Had Card In Possession But Transaction Unauthorized	313/ 169	11.1 / 11.0	313/ 169	100.0%/100.0%
3. A/H Withdrew Against Insufficient/Bad Deposit Causing Overdraft)	51/ 13	1.8 / 0.9	51/ 13	100.0%/100.0%
4. A/H Confused — No Error	235/ 194	8.3 / 12.6	0/ 0	0.0%/ 0.0%
5. Bank's Computer Was Off-Line (Causing Overdraft)	171/ 13	6.1 / 0.9	171/ 13	100.0%/100.0%
6. Bank's Delayed Posting Procedure (Causing Overdraft)	10/ 24	0.3 / 1.6	10/ 24	100.0%/100.0%
7. Bank's ATM Had Mechanical Problem (Causing Short/Over Or Wrong Posting)	579/ 469	20.6 / 30.6	0/ 0	0.0%/ 0.0%
8. Other	66/ 22	2.3 / 1.4	12/ 2	18.2%/ 9.1%
SUBTOTAL	2069/1208	73.4 / 78.8	1201/525	58.0%/ 43.5%
Deposit-Related:				
9. A/H Deposited Empty Envelope	29/ 13	1.0 / 0.9	17/ 4	58.6%/ 30.8%
10. A/H Deposited In Wrong Account	50/ 35	1.8 / 2.3	0/ 0	0.0%/ 0.0%
11. A/H Deposited Amount Different Than That Indicated On Envelope And/Or That Keyed Into ATM	43/ 33	1.5 / 2.1	0/ 0	0.0%/ 0.0%
12. A/H Deposited Stolen/Fraudulent Check	10/ 3	0.3 / 0.2	10/ 3	100.0%/100.0%
13. A/H Deposited Uncollectible (Other Than Stolen/Fraudulent) Check	25/ 10	0.9 / 0.6	14/ 0	56.0%/ 0.0%
14. A/H Confused — No Error	137/ 31	4.9 / 2.0	0/ 0	0.0%/ 0.0%
15. Bank Posted Incorrect Amount	42/ 57	1.5 / 3.7	0/ 1	0.0%/ 1.8%
16. Bank Posted To Wrong Account	24/ 9	0.9 / 0.6	0/ 0	0.0%/ 0.0%
17. Person Other Than A/H Made Bad Deposit	76/ 39	2.7 / 2.5	76/ 39	100.0%/100.0%
18. Other	36/ 32	1.3 / 2.1	2/ 1	5.6%/ 3.1%
SUBTOTAL	472/ 262	16.8 / 17.0	119/ 48	25.2%/ 18.3%
19. Unreported	276/ 64	9.8 / 4.2	19/ 3	6.9%/ 4.7%
TOTAL NUMBER OF CAUSES*	2817/1534	100.0%/100.0%	1339/576	47.5%/37.6%
TOTAL NUMBER OF DISTINCT INCIDENTS INVOLVED*	2707/1480	-- / --	1216/527	44.9%/35.6%

*Each incident can have one or more causes.

42

Exhibit 3.8

ATM: Incidents by Type of Initial Complaint and Potential to be Fradulent

Initial Complaint	ATM Incidents (1983/1984)		Potentially Fraudulent Incidents (1983/1984)	
	Number	Column %	Number	Row %
Accountholder-Initiated:				
1. Unauthorized Withdrawal	1189/ 618	43.9%/ 41.8%	921/472	77.5%/ 76.4%
2. Short (Due to Dispensing)	603/ 487	22.3 / 32.9	3/ 0	0.5%/ 0.0%
3. Deposit Not Credited	441/ 162	16.3 / 10.9	1/ 1	0.2%/ 0.6%
4. Short (Due to Posting)	81/ 79	3.0 / 5.3	2/ 0	2.5%/ 0.0%
5. Deposit Credited, But Erroneously	63/ 54	2.3 / 3.7	0/ 0	0.0%/ 0.0%
6. Other	36/ 4	1.3 / 0.3	12/ 0	33.3%/ 0.0%
SUBTOTAL	2413/1404	89.1 / 74.9	939/473	38.9%/ 33.7%
Bank-Initiated:				
7. Overdraft	194/ 57	7.2 / 3.9	187/ 48	96.4%/ 84.2%
8. Stolen/Fraudulent Check Deposited	47/ 2	1.7 / 0.1	44/ 2	93.6%/100.0%
9. Empty Envelope Deposited	31/ 6	1.1 / 0.4	28/ 4	90.3%/ 66.7%
10. Uncollectible (Other Than Stolen/ Fraudulent) Check Deposited	15/ 8	0.6 / 0.5	15/ 0	100.0%/ 0.0%
11. Other	5/ 3	0.2 / 0.2	2/ 0	40.0%/ 0.0%
SUBTOTAL	292/ 76	10.8 / 5.1	276/ 54	94.5%/ 71.1%
12. Unreported	2/ 0	0.1 / --	1/ --	50.0%/ --
TOTAL	2707/1480	100.0%/100.0%	1216/527	44.9%/ 35.6%

the potentially fraudulent proportion is consistent over the two years worth of unauthorized withdrawals again supports our earlier claim that within a complaint category the data is quite representative. Another noteworthy statistic in Exhibit 3.8 is the high proportion of bank-initiated incidents that are determined to be potentially fraudulent; unfortunately, as noted earlier, this type of incidents is underrepresented in our sample of incidents.

Exhibit 3.9 displays the dollar amounts of claim by the accountholder and the bank for the potentially fraudulent incidents; it should be compared with Exhibit 3.4, which displays corresponding figures for all the ATM incidents. As expected, the potentially fraudulent incidents involve larger dollar amounts. In 1984, for example, the average accountholder claim for all unauthorized withdrawal incidents (see Exhibit 3.4) is $301, while the corresponding figure for the potentially fraudulent, unauthorized withdrawal incidents (see Exhibit 3.9) is $351, implying that the average amount claimed for the not potentially fraudulent, unauthorized withdrawal incidents is only $153. Interestingly, except for those instances with inadequately small sample sizes, the average claims are comparable for the two years of study.

Lost or Stolen Cards

Exhibit 3.7 clearly suggests that lost or stolen cards constitute the majority of the potentially fraudulent incidents. Because of the importance of this cause of ATM fraud, several lost or stolen card-related issues are discussed in this subsection and are summarized in the eight-part Exhibit 3.10.

How Do Accountholders Lose Possession of Their Cards?

Exhibit 3.10(a) shows that cards are most often reported stolen, as opposed to lost or never received. 63.6 percent of the 644 incidents and 73.3 percent of the 304 incidents involving lost or stolen cards were reported stolen in 1983 and 1984, respectively. There are typically four ways in which a card may be stolen:

(i)   Larceny. Theft of an ATM card with the PIN could be by a relative, friend or other person with access to the accountholder's residence, place of employment, or car. This least confrontational and most prevalent means of obtaining the card and PIN is a form of larceny. Another form of larceny includes pick-pocketing and purse-snatching.

(ii)   Burglary. If the theft of the card and PIN is prefaced with the breaking and entering of the accountholder's residence, place of employment, or car, then it is classified as a burglary. As discussed later, the card and PIN might be either the direct target or the by-product of the burglary.

(iii)   Confidence Game. It is not surprising that confidence games

have been used to fraudulently obtain ATM cards and PINs. The following incident, which occurred in 1983, typifies an ATM con game. A man peers over the shoulder of a woman making a withdrawal at an ATM and notices her PIN as she keys it in. A few moments later, as the woman is completing her transaction, the man distracts her by starting a conversation, thus allowing his partner to take the woman's card as it comes out of the ATM. When the woman turns to retrieve her card and finds it missing, the man explains that the ATM has been malfunctioning recently and has "eaten" several cards. The two con men, now possessing both the woman's card and her PIN, proceeded to withdraw all $500 from her account.

(iv)   Robbery. Accountholders are becoming increasingly concerned about being robbed of their cards and PINs, especially those living in large urban areas with high crime rates. Such incidents are freqently reported in the local media, thus further heightening the crime concerns of the public [American Banker, 1984]. In the case of a residential robbery, the perpetrator would regard the card and PIN as valuables worth taking from the accountholder. If the PIN is not written down, the robber could also use force to obtain the PIN from the accountholder. In another scenario, an accountholder, especially an elderly person using an ATM at night, is an inviting target for a robbery. Even if the ATM has a camera, the robber could force the accountholder to make a withdrawal.

Cards are reported lost less frequently than they are reported stolen. The percentage lost may in fact be even lower, since a card may actually have been stolen even though the accountholder reported it lost. For example, if an accountholder discovers that his card is missing from his wallet, he might assume that he lost the card when in fact it was stolen, unbeknownst to him.

In less than 10 percent of the lost or stolen card incidents, the accountholders reported that they never received their cards. Closer examination of these incidents reveals that the cards are most often stolen while in transit from the bank to the accountholder's residence. The vast majority of our Panel banks mail the card and PIN separately to the accountholder, which, it should be noted, from a risk-to-fraud perspective, is less vulnerable than mailing the card and PIN together, but more vulnerable than requiring the accountholder to pick up the card and PIN at the bank.

Where Are The Cards Lost or Stolen?

As indicated in Exhibit 3.10(b), the home is the most common place where the card is lost or stolen, reflecting the frequent occurrence of residential larcenies, burglaries, and robberies. Cards are also

Exhibit 3.9

ATM: Potentially Fraudulent Incidents By Amount of Claim

Initial Complaint	Number of Potentially Fraudulent Incidents (1983/1984)	Incidents Reporting A Claim (1983/1984)			
		Accountholder Claim		Bank Claim	
		Number	$Average	Number	$Average
Accountholder-Initiated:					
1. Unauthorized Withdrawal	921/472	893/418	$322/$351	43/18	$288/$527
2. Short (Due to Dispensing)	3/ 0	3/ —	$ 13/—	0/ —	—/ —
3. Deposit Not Credited	1/ 1	1/ 1	$238/$100	0/ 0	—/ —
4. Short (Due to Posting)	2/ 0	2/ —	$110/—	0/ —	—/ —
5. Deposit Credited, But Erroneously	0/ 0	—/ —	—/ —	—/ —	—/ —
6. Other	12/ 0	10/ —	$303/—	1/ —	$ 25/—
SUBTOTAL	939/473	909/419	$320/$350	44/18	$282/$527
Bank-Initiated:					
7. Overdraft	187/ 48	11/ 1	$846/$ 1	179/44	$ 233/$268
8. Stolen/Fraudulent Check Deposited	44/ 2	4/ 0	$292/—	32/ 0	$1023/—
9. Empty Envelope Deposited	28/ 4	8/ 0	$228/—	18/ 3	$ 282/$828
10. Uncollectible (Other Than Stolen/Fraudulent) Check Deposited	15/ 0	1/ —	$200/—	13/ —	$ 705/—
11. Other	2/ 0	2/ —	$100/—	0/ —	—/ —
SUBTOTAL	276/ 54	26/ 1	$488/$ 1	242/47	$ 368/$304
12. Unreported	1/ 0	0/ —	—/ —	1/ —	$ 15/—
TOTAL	1216/527	935/420	$325/$349	287/65	$ 354/$366

45

Exhibit 3.10

ATM: Potentially Fraudulent Incidents Involving Lost or Stolen Cards

Category	1983/1984 (N=644/304)
Card Stolen	63.6%/ 73.3%
Card Lost	27.2 / 19.3
Card Never Received	9.2 / 7.4
TOTAL	100.0%/100.0%

(a) How Accountholders Lose Possession of Cards

Location	1983/1984 (N=395/183)
Home	24.8%/ 31.1%
Retail Establishment	20.0 / 12.6
Car	18.0 / 13.7
Place of Employment	12.4 / 10.4
Street	8.4 / 12.6
School	6.9 / 2.7
Other Place	9.5 / 16.9
TOTAL	100.0%/100.0%

(b) Location of Loss or Theft of Card

Category	1983/1984 (N=379/205)
Only Card Taken	26.1%/ 33.2%
Card and Purse/Wallet Taken	66.0 / 53.7
Card, Purse/Wallet and Other Items Taken	7.9 / 13.1
TOTAL	100.0%/100.0%

(c) Nature of Theft

Exhibit 3.10

(Page 2 of 3)

Exposure Time	1983/1984 (N=260/142)
Time Elapsed Before Accountholder Discovers Card Missing (Days):	
0	90.8%/ 75.2%
1-7	7.2 / 15.5
>7	2.0 / 9.2
Total	100.0%/100.0%
Time Elapsed Between Discovery and Bank Notification (Days):	
0-2	74.4 / 86.0
>2	25.6 / 14.0
Total	100.0%/100.0%

(d) Exposure Time of a Lost or Stolen Card

Location	1983/1984 (N=437/206)
On Card	5.7%/ 2.9%
Near Card (In Purse/Wallet)	72.3 / 47.6
Written Elsewhere	6.9 / 22.3
Not Written Down	15.1 / 27.2
TOTAL	100.0%/100.0%

(e) Location of Personal Identification Number (PIN)

47

Exhibit 3.10

(Page 3 of 3)

PIN Disclosed To:	1983/1984 (N=252/188)
Family/Friend	23.4 / 16.0%
Other Person Known to Accountholder	3.2 / 2.7
Person Impersonating Bank Official	3.6 / 2.1
Other Person Unknown to Accountholder	5.6 / 2.7
No One	64.2 / 76.5
TOTAL	100.0%/100.0%

(f) Disclosure of PIN

Days Between Last Transaction and Bank Notification	1983/1984 (N=440/183)
Last Transaction Before Bank Notification	48.4%/ 43.2%
0	38.2 / 40.4
>0	13.4 / 16.4
TOTAL	100.0%/100.0%

(g) Use of a Lost or Stolen Card

Number of Withdrawals	1983/1984 (N=535/241)
1	27.1%/ 23.7%
2	23.6 / 14.9
3-5	28.2 / 33.2
6-10	12.9 / 19.1
>10	8.2 / 9.1
TOTAL	100.0%/100.0%

(h) Number of Withdrawals Made with a Lost or Stolen Card

frequently lost or stolen in retail establishments, cars, places of employment, streets, and schools.

How Are The Cards Stolen?

Exhibit 3.10(c) indicates that in a majority of the incidents involving stolen cards, the theft of the card is the indirect result of a theft of a purse/wallet or of a more general theft where the purse/wallet and other items are taken. Yet, at the same time, Exhibit 3.10(c) also indicates that ATM cards are increasingly becoming the direct target of thefts. In 1983, 26.1 percent of the 379 incidents involving stolen cards resulted in only the card being stolen. The percentage increased to 33.2 percent in 1984. While this increase may not be statistically significant, it does suggest a trend that should be carefully monitored.

What Is The Exposure Time of A Lost or Stolen Card?

The exposure time of a lost or stolen card can be defined as the elapsed time from when the card is first missing to when the card can no longer be used to make transactions. In a sense, this quantity is indicative of the potential for fraudulent abuse: the longer the exposure time, the greater is the potential for abuse.

The exposure time of a lost or stolen ATM card depends to a large degree on how quickly the accountholder (i) realizes the cards is missing, and (ii) reports the missing card to the bank. Records of only 260 of the 644 1983 and 142 of the 304 1984 lost or stolen card incidents contained the three relevant dates: the date the card was actually missing, the date the card was discovered missing, and the date the card was reported missing to the bank. Exhibit 3.10(d) shows that, fortunately, accountholders frequently discover that the card is missing on the same day that it was actually missing. In many of the incidents in which several days had elapsed between the date the card was actually missing and the date the card was discovered missing, the bank had to inform the accountholder that something was amiss (e.g., an overdraft caused by insufficient funds).

Turning to how quickly accountholders report the card missing once it is discovered missing, Exhibit 3.10(d) indicates that in 1984, as compared to 1983, the accountholders took less time to inform the bank of their missing card. The percentage of incidents in which the accountholders reported the card missing within two days of discovery -- thereby limiting their liability under Reg E to $50 -- increased from 74.4 percent in 1983 to 86.0 percent in 1984. Examination of the incidents in which the reporting delay was more than two days reveals that they are often attributable to accountholder ignorance. For example, some accountholders reported the theft to the local police, and only as an after thought and at a later time did they report it to the bank.

While the exposure time of a missing ATM card greatly depends on the accountholder promptly informing the bank, it should be noted that exposure time also depends on the

speed in which the bank "hot cards" the missing card. Many of our Panel banks have a 24-hour on-line hot carding system, meaning that there is the capability for immediately hot carding a missing card, once it is reported missing. Other Panel banks only have on-line hot carding during business hours, and they perform "batch" hot carding on those cards reported missing after business hours. Unfortunately, small sample sizes precluded us from analyzing the impact of on-line -- versus batch -- hot carding. Nevertheless, it is reasonable to assume that on-line hot carding tends to shorten the exposure time, and hereby reduce the potential for card abuse.

Where Are the Personal Identification Numbers (PINs) Kept?

Inasmuch as the Panel banks only provided those lost or stolen incidents in which the card was used fraudulently, it is not known how many cards were lost or stolen but not subsequently used because the PIN was not known to the person possessing the card. Yet in a large majority of the lost or stolen card incidents, the person possessing the card knew the PIN because it was written down on or near the card (see Exhibit 3.10(e)), indicating that many accountholders compromise the security of the PIN, which, it should be noted, is the bank's principal "front-end" security measure (i.e., a control designed to restrict access to an account).

Why are so many accountholders negligent regarding the safety of their PINs? Perhaps, accountholders have difficulty remembering their PINs; this is not unreasonable, especially if the PIN is a bank-assigned random number. Does this observation imply that bank-assigned PINs are inherently riskier than customer-selected PINs? Not necessarily. On the one hand, accountholders certainly have less trouble remembering a self-selected PIN than a bank-assigned PIN. But, on the other hand, a self-selected PIN is frequently easy to guess, as it is usually a name, a phone number, or other identifier that is contained in the accountholder's purse or wallet. Inasmuch as an ATM generally allows several attempts to enter the correct PIN before capturing the card, it is possible that the PIN could be guessed if it were self-selected, rather than bank-assigned.

Finally, a somewhat positive observation can be made in Exhibit 3.10(e): accountholders were less likely to write their PIN down on or near the card in 1984 than in 1983. Again, this initial observation should be monitored to see if it develops into a trend.

Are PINs Disclosed To Others?

In addition to writing down their PINs, many accountholders disclose their PINs to other people, again despite bank warnings to the contrary. Exhibit 3.10(f) shows that the PINs are quite often revealed to family members or friends. In these instances, the PIN is usually revealed either in a casual conversation or because the accountholder wants the person to perform an ATM transaction for him/her. In one incident, an accountholder, after giving her son her card to make a withdrawal, yelled out the PIN as he was leaving the house. A group of neighborhood youths playing in the yard heard her; one of them later entered the house, took the card, performed withdrawals, and then returned the card to the house.

The accountholder, however, is not always negligent in the PIN's disclosure. Exhibit 3.10(f) indicates that in a small percentage of incidents, the PIN was disclosed to someone impersonating a bank official. As another example in which no accountholder negligence is present, the PIN could be forcefully obtained, as in the case of a robbery.

How Extensively Are Lost or Stolen Cards Used?

A lost or stolen ATM card cannot, of course, be used without the appropriate PIN. Other limitations to the card's use include the amount of funds in the accountholder's bank account and the bank's operating procedures. Typically, the maximum amount of funds a user can withdrawal per day is set by the bank at between $200 and $300. Banks sometimes also limit the number of withdrawals per day.

Interestingly, Exhibit 3.10(g) shows that in nearly half the incidents involving a lost or stolen card, the last transaction was made prior to the bank being notified of the card's missing status. Thus, accountholders should be constantly aware of the status of their ATM card, so that they may report its loss or theft in a timely manner. Exhibit 3.10(g) also shows that in 13.4 percent of the 440 1983 incidents and 16.4 percent of the 183 1984 incidents the last transaction was made at least one day after the accountholder reported the card missing, indicating that the card was not "hot carded" promptly. This situation could have occurred either because bank personnel did not follow bank procedures or because of the inherent limitations in the procedures themselves (e.g., the bank can only hot card during business hours).

The number of withdrawals made with a lost or stolen card is also of interest. While Exhibit 3.10(h) contains the complete distribution of the number of withdrawals made with a lost or stolen card, the average number of withdrawals made was 4.2 and 4.7 in 1983 and 1984, respectively. Correspondingly, the dollar value of these withdrawals was $437 and $419 in 1983 and 1984, respectively.

Suspected Perpetrator

The identity of the perpetrator in ATM frauds is important just as it is in other types of frauds and crimes. In addition to resolving the ATM fraud, the identity of the perpetrator provides insight into whether the fraud is opportunistic in nature and whether "front-end" security measures could be effective. Unfortunately, except in the few cases where the perpetrator has confessed or the ATM camera has an unmistakable picture of the perpetrator, the identity of the perpetrator is usually difficult to ascertain; instead, a suspected perpetrator is sometimes indicated in the incident report.

Exhibit 3.11 examines the identity of the perpetrator for the two leading causes of withdrawal-related incidents -- the incidents involving a lost or stolen card and the incidents involving an unauthorized withdrawal in which the accountholder claims that he/she is still in possession of the card. Overall, in less than one third of the incidents was the perpetrator identified or suspected. Interestingly, the most frequently identified or suspected perpetrator was the accountholder, especially in cases in which the accountholder was still in possession of the card. It is clear that in these cases, front-end security measures (e.g., PINs) are of no value because it is the accountholder, the authorized user, who is suspected of committing the fraud. In an additional 16.3 percent of the 957 1983 incidents and 12.9 percent of the 473 1984 incidents, family members, friends or acquaintances of the accountholder were identified as or suspected to be the perpetrator. Actually, out of the incidents for which a perpetrator was suspected or identified, the perpetrator was thought to be the accountholder or someone related to him/her in 89.3 percent and 96.1 percent of such incidents in 1983 and 1984, respectively.

How effective are cameras in identifying ATM perpetrators? Focusing on the Exhibit 3.11 incidents, we examined whether a photograph was available and, if so, whether the perpetrator could be identified. Reflecting the fact that only a few of the ATMs of the Panel banks are camera-equipped, a photograph was available in 23.3 percent of the 957 1983 incidents and in 1.1 percent of the 473 1984 incidents. In further analyzing the larger 1983 data set, it was determined that even when a photograph was available, the perpetrator was subsequently identified in only 36.7 percent of the time. Thus, equipping all the ATMs with cameras is probably not a long term solution to ATM fraud, since there are many ways to "fool" the camera. Equipping some ATMs with cameras, on the other hand, may be a cost-effective strategy, as there is an element of chance as to whether or not a particular ATM is equipped with a camera.

Financial Disposition

In addition to an ATM incident's initial complaint, amount of claim, complaint cause, potential for fraudulence, lost or stolen card, and suspected perpetrator, the other key component of an incident is its financial disposition. In particular, for the potentially fraudulent incidents, what is the disposition of the financial claims indicated in Exhibit 3.9? In each incident, the accountholder and/or the bank can make a financial claim. If the accountholder makes a claim, the bank can honor (i.e., pay) any part, or all, of the claim, within the guidelines stipulated by Reg E. Likewise, if the bank makes a claim, it might recover from the accountholder and/or perpetrator any part, or all, of the claim. Although it is clear when the bank loses money in an incident, many times it is difficult to determine whether or not the accountholder actually lost money if the bank denied his/her claim, particularly in those incidents in which the perpetrators were unknown. Therefore, an accountholder's "loss" in Exhibit 3.12 refers to a loss that is relative to the accountholder's claim (e.g., a

Exhibit 3.11

ATM: Potentially Fraudulent Withdrawal-Related Incidents By Identity Of Perpetrator And Card Status

Identity of Perpetrator	Accountholder Claims (1983/1984)					
	"Card In Possession"		"Card Lost/Stolen"		Total	
	Number	Column %	Number	Column %	Number	Column %
Suspected Or Identified To Be:						
Accountholder (A/H)	84/ 63	26.8%/ 37.3%	12/ 0	1.8%/ 0.0%	96/ 63	10.0%/ 13.3%
Spouse Or Child Of A/H	29/ 8	9.3 / 4.7	26/ 10	4.0 / 3.3	55/ 18	5.8 / 3.8
Boy/Girl Friend Of A/H	9/ 8	2.9 / 4.7	10/ 8	1.6 / 2.6	19/ 16	2.0 / 3.4
Other Relationship To A/H	27/ 8	8.6 / 4.7	54/ 19	8.4 / 6.3	81/ 27	8.5 / 5.7
No Relation to A/H	1/ 0	0.3 / 0.0	29/ 5	4.5 / 1.6	30/ 5	3.1 / 1.1
Subtotal	150/ 87	47.9 / 51.5	131/ 42	20.3 / 13.8	281/129	29.4 / 27.3
Unknown	150/ 44	47.9 / 26.0	481/192	74.7 / 63.2	631/236	65.9 / 49.9
Unreported	13/ 38	4.2/ 22.5	32/ 70	5.0 / 23.0	45/108	4.7 / 22.8
Total	313/169	100.0%/100.0%	644/304	100.0%/100.0%	957/473	100.0%/100.0%

Exhibit 3.12

ATM: Potentially Fraudulent Incidents By Financial Disposition and Number of Transactions

Financial Disposition	Total Sample (1983/1984)		Average "Loss" (1983/1984) Sustained by:		Average Number of Transactions (1983/1984)
	Number	Column %	Bank	Accountholder	
No "Loss" Involved	45/ 12	3.8% / 2.3%	$ 0/$ 0	$ 0/$ 0	2.2/1.9
Accountholder "Loss" Only	369/152	30.3 / 28.8	$ 0/$ 0	$255/$304	3.5/4.1
Bank "Loss" Only	446/179	36.7 / 34.0	$330/$350	$ 0/$ 0	3.3/3.3
Both Accountholder "Loss" and Bank "Loss"	202/ 97	16.6 / 18.4	$365/$363	$ 74/$ 53	4.8/5.1
Unreported	153/ 87	12.6 / 16.5	-- / --	-- / --	-- / --
TOTAL	1216/527	100.0%/100.0%	$208/$222	$103/$117	3.6/3.9

denial of a claim by the bank implies that the accountholder sustained a "loss" equal to the amount of his/her claim).

The financial dispositions tabulated in Exhibit 3.12 clearly indicate that the 1983 figures are quite comparable to the corresponding 1984 figures; they also suggest that it is rare that a potentially fraudulent incident involves no loss. A no loss incident implies that a full recovery has been made (e.g., the bank receives full restitution for an overdraft). In incidents involving only losses to the accountholder, the average loss was $255 in 1983 and $304 in 1984. Accountholder claims are denied for a variety of reasons, the most common of which are listed in Exhibit 3.13. An accountholder having his/her card in possession is the overwhelming reason for denying an accountholder claim, followed by the reason that the accountholder is confused or withdraws the claim. Interestingly, despite the fact that Reg E explicitly states that the assessment of liability is independent of the PIN status, some banks are denying claims because of the PIN's presumed status. While some accountholders are denied credit for revealing their PINs, other accountholders have their claims denied because they insisted that their PINs had been secure and had not been revealed to anyone. In these latter incidents, the banks reason that if the PIN had indeed been secure, as the accountholder stated, then the accountholder is the only possible person who could have performed the transaction; hence, the accountholder is suspected and his/her claim is denied, leading to an accountholder "loss".

Returning to Exhibit 3.12, we see that "bank loss only" was the most common type of financial disposition in both 1983 and 1984. The average bank loss was $330 in 1983 and $350 in 1984. While some of the bank loss incidents are due to overdrafts by accountholders who abscond with the funds, others involve accountholder claims that are paid in full by the bank, including many claims that could have been reduced by an amount equal to the Reg E liability. For reasons of customer relations, banks are sometimes loathe to assess the Reg E liability.

The vast majority of the 202 incidents in 1983 and the 97 incidents in 1984 in which both the accountholder and the bank sustained a loss, involved the bank paying all the accountholder's claim except for the Reg E liability, which is either $50 (if the accountholder reports the card missing to the bank within two days of discovering it missing) or $500 (if the accountholder reports the card missing more than two days after discovering it missing). Thus, the average accountholder loss of $74 in 1983 and $53 in 1984 primarily reflects the amount of assessed Reg E liability. The average bank loss of $365 in 1983 and $363 in 1984 in these incidents suggest their seriousness. Not surprisingly and as indicated in Exhibit 3.12, the seriousness of an incident is also suggested by the number of transactions; that is, the total loss sustained by the accountholder and the bank in an incident is somewhat proportional to the number of

transactions carried out as a part of the incident.

For all the potentially fraudulent incidents, the average bank loss was $208 in 1983 and $222 in 1984. While these figures are not likely to cause great concern at large banks, it should be pointed out that a number of such small losses can quickly add up to a large total loss. Moreover, there is the potential for large single-incident bank losses. In our incident sample, the largest single incident loss was $5,950 in 1983 and $8,070 in 1984.

Reg E

As noted earlier, some banks do not assess the Reg E liability. Yet, it is well known that bankers are dissatisfied with Reg E, which was made law in 1978, at the crest of the pro-consumer movement that swept the Nation in the late seventies. In particular, many bankers claim that the law encourages irresponsible behavior on the part of accountholders and makes it too easy for dishonest accountholders to defraud banks [Weinstein, 1985(b)]. Although the validity of this claim can only be assessed in light of an extensive survey of accountholders, it is, as noted earlier in Exhibit 3.11, a fact that bankers do suspect the accountholder in a number of incidents.

Our sample of ATM incidents does, however, show that banks are paying for some accountholder negligence, especially in incidents involving lost or stolen cards and when the PIN is revealed or written down next to the card. In fact, the Office of the Comptroller of the Currency, the agency that regulates national banks, has expressed concern over banks which illegally (i.e., in violation of Reg E) warn their cardholders that they are liable for losses resulting from unauthorized transactions when they reveal their PINs [EFTA, 1985(b)]. On the other hand, is it the intention of Reg E to protect the accountholder even when he/she is negligent? If so, then bank loss due to accountholder negligence should be added to the list of elements -- including "data processing, labor and administration" -- that the Federal Reserve Board [1984] found were the most costly to the banks in their efforts to comply with Reg E.

3.3 EXTENT OF ATM FRAUD

Whereas the previous section focused on the nature of ATM incidents, the purpose of this section is to project nationwide bank losses that could be attributable to ATM fraud. In order to make this projection and as indicated in Section 3.1, it was necessary to determine the ATM fraud loss for each Panel bank and then to normalize it by an appropriate base (i.e., number of ATM transactions and dollar volume of ATM transactions). Consistent loss ratios (i.e., loss per transaction and loss per $1,000 volume of transaction) were then determined, and nationwide projections were made by multiplying each ratio by the nationwide estimate for the corresponding base variable in the ratio. Before discussing the loss ratios and the nationwide estimates, it should

Exhibit 3.13

ATM: Reasons An Accountholder's Claim Is Denied In A Potentially Fraudulent Incident

Reason For Denial	Potentially Fraudulent Incidents (1983/1984) (N=356/132)
Accountholder (A/H) Confused Or Withdraws Claim	15.2% / 6.0%
A/H Had Card In Possession	53.7 / 72.0
A/H Revealed PIN To Person	11.2 / 12.1
A/H Claimed PIN Was Secure	5.9 / 1.5
A/H Could Not Provide Sufficient Information	5.9 / 2.3
Bank Had No Record Of Transaction	0.3 / —
Other	7.8 / 6.1
TOTAL	100.0% / 100.0%

be noted that while the ATM loss figure for a bank could be determined by summing the bank losses for the individual incidents, it was not possible to do so in this study since the obtained incidents represented only a sample of all incidents.

Loss Ratios

Exhibit 3.14(a) contains the various loss ratios. After computing, say, loss per transaction for each individual Panel bank, the lowest, the average, and the highest figures for this ratio were identified and entered in Exhibit 3.14(a). Why not just provide an overall average for the Panel banks? One reason is that inasmuch as the Panel banks may not be representative of all commercial banks, such an average would be misleading. Another reason is to highlight the fact that each ratio can possess a wide range of values.

Several comments should be made concerning Exhibit 3.14(a). First, it should be noted that the 1983 and 1984 loss ratios within a particular loss figure category -- say, the low figure category -- are not necessarily associated with the same Panel bank. Second, as might be expected, the low and high figures belong, for the most part, to the smaller and larger Panel banks, respectively. Third, again as might be expected, the low and high figures for each ratio differ considerably, by a factor of several hundred to several thousand. Fourth, the 1984 figures are generally lower than the corresponding 1983 figures -- is this significant? The answer is no -- we attribute it to both the year-to-year fluctuations and the instability in the underlying measure (which is a ratio of two random quantities).

Nationwide Estimates

Multiplying the bank loss ratios in Exhibit 3.14(a) with the corresponding estimates for the base variable yielded the nationwide loss figures tabulated in Exhibit 3.14(b). The base variable estimates were based on our analysis of the transaction trend and our assumption that the average dollar value per transaction has remained constant -- at $97 -- for the years 1983 and 1984; our estimates differ somewhat from Zimmer's estimates (which are tabulated in Exhibit 1.3). Again, as in the case of the loss ratios, we have indicated in Exhibit 3.14(b) the low, average and high nationwide estimates. By way of explanation, the high figure of $212.9M for 1984 represents nationwide bank loss that might be expected if, on the average, all banks showed the characteristics and anticipated losses of the Panel bank with the highest loss per transaction volume in 1984.

Given the collection of figures in Exhibit 3.14(b), the question still remains as to what is the best estimate for the nationwide ATM bank loss? In (i) reviewing the underlying Panel characteristics, (ii) recognizing that most of the installed ATMs belong to the larger commercial banks (which, as indicated earlier, tend to have the higher loss ratios), and (iii) looking at both the 1983 and 1984 figures, it is reasonable to state that the nationwide ATM bank loss --

based on the 1983 and 1984 data sets -- is between $70 and $100 million per year. This estimated range clearly indicates that we consider the average figures in Exhibit 3.14(b) to be low for the nationwide estimate; indeed, the $70 million to $100 million annual loss is what might be expected if, on the average, all banks were like the Panel bank possessing the median loss ratios.

Although $70 to $100 million may seem large, it is less than 0.03 percent of the $291 billion transaction volume in 1984. Further, it is significantly less than the $561 million annual fraud loss which Nilson [1985] has estimated for the credit card industry. One possible explanation for this difference in fraud loss is that organized fraud, especially card counterfeiting operations, currently plaguing the credit card industry does not appear to be a problem at this time in the ATM industry. Instead, ATM frauds are still opportunistic in nature.

Another approach to comparing the fraud loss in ATM cards to that of credit cards is by focusing on the pertinent loss ratios, as is done in Exhibit 3.15. Interestingly, while five years ago Mastercard's fraud loss ratios were three to four times lower than VISA's, today the two organizations have comparable loss ratios. Also, the year-to-year variation in the loss ratios for the credit card companies should be noted, suggesting that the 1983-to-1984 variation in the ATM loss ratios is not without precedent. In particular, the drop in the ATM loss ratios should not be interpreted as a trend. In comparing the ATM and credit card loss ratios, we see that on a loss per transaction basis, ATM fraud losses are five to six times lower than credit card fraud losses. The relative difference is even larger in the loss per $1000 of transaction category. Limited credit card fraud data supplied by a few of our Panel banks also indicates that their credit card fraud losses differ from their ATM fraud losses by factors consistent with the differences observed in Exhibit 3.15.

A final question can be asked: will the nationwide bank loss due to ATM fraud increase in the next few years? Certainly, as noted earlier, the two years worth of ATM fraud data cannot establish a trend. However, like Mastercard, ATM fraud losses might increase as the ATM industry matures; indeed, the estimated ATM loss per transaction in 1983 approximates that for Mastercard in 1979. While the ATM fraud losses might follow the recent upward trend observed in the credit card industry, it is, of course, hoped that this would not be the case, especially if appropriate fraud prevention measures can be implemented. The findings of this pilot effort should help in identifying such measures.

Exhibit 3.14

ATM: Fraud Loss Ratios and Nationwide Estimates

	Loss Amount (1983/1984)		
	Low Figure	Average Figure	High Figure
Loss Per Transaction (i.e., Withdrawal or Deposit)	$0.0001/$0.0001	$0.0189/$0.0154	$0.0731/$0.0583
Loss Per $1000 of Transaction Volume	$0.0004/$0.0009	$0.2269/$0.1783	$1.1218/$0.7315

(a) ATM Fraud Loss Ratios

	Nationwide Loss Estimates (1983/1984)		
	Low Figure	Average Figure	High Figure
Based on Estimate of 2.7B/3.0B Transactions in 1983/1984.	$0.3M/$0.3M	$51.0M/$46.2M	$197.4M/$174.9M
Based on Estimate of $262B/$291B in Transaction Volume in 1983/1984.	$0.1M/$0.3M	$59.4M/$51.9M	$294.0M/$212.9M

(b) Nationwide ATM Fraud Loss Estimates

56

Exhibit 3.15

ATM: Comparison of Fraud Losses With Those For Credit Cards

Year	Loss Per Transaction			Loss Per $1000 of Volume		
	VISA[1]	Mastercard[2]	ATM[3]	VISA[1]	Mastercard[2]	ATM[3]
1979	$0.066	$0.018	----	$1.699	$0.496	----
1980	0.075	0.030	----	1.799	0.763	----
1981	0.071	0.042	----	1.600	0.989	----
1982	0.081	0.075	----	1.701	1.634	----
1983	0.081	0.074	$0.019	1.590	1.441	$0.227
1984	0.088	0.080	0.015	1.601	1.450	0.178

Sources: [1]"Visa Turning the Cards on Fraud", VISA, San Francisco, February, 1984; Telephone Conversation with VISA Spokesperson, June 7, 1985.

[2]Telephone Conversation with Mastercard Spokesperson, February 13, 1985.

[3]See Exhibit 3.14(a) for average figures.

4 WIRE TRANSFER FRAUD

In this section, our emphasis changes from the primary retail EFT technology, ATMs, to the primary corporate EFT technology, wire transfer. Not surprisingly, frauds in the two technologies are quite different. One major difference is that while ATM incidents occur frequently, with the largest banks experiencing several thousand incidents per year, wire transfer incidents are rare, with even the largest banks experiencing only a few incidents per year. Another difference is that while ATM incidents involve small amounts of money, the exposure in a wire transfer incident may be quite large -- in the millions of dollars. A third difference is that while Reg E requires detailed documentation of ATM incidents that involve accountholder complaints, there is no formal mechanism for documenting wire transfer incidents, which are typically recorded in an ad hoc manner. A fourth difference is that while banks are concerned about ATM incidents, they are quite fearful of wire transfer incidents. All these differences are highlighted in Sections 4.1 and 4.2, where we discuss pertinent data collection issues and the nature of wire transfer fraud, respectively.

As in the case of ATM fraud, we also attempted to assess the extent of wire transfer fraud -- to this end, we developed the Wire Transfer: Summary Data Collection Instrument (see Exhibit A.4). Unfortunately, the attempt was hampered by a lack of available data. Thus, the extent of wire transfer fraud is not addressed in this report, except to note in Section 5.3 that it is an important area for future study. We were able, however, to complement our collection of wire transfer incidents with a survey of wire transfer managers -- their attitudes toward wire transfer fraud are discussed in Section 4.3.

4.1 DATA COLLECTION ISSUES

The data collection issues and problems discussed in Section 3.1 for the ATM area are compounded in the wire transfer area, primarily because of two aforementioned facts -- wire transfer incidents are rare and there is no formal mechanism for documenting them. Errors or inquires concerning wire transfers are usually kept on a log, while documentation of incidents requiring further investigation or legal action are kept in folders that might be in the possession of the bank's wire transfer manager, its security office, or its audit and control office. Inasmuch as domestic and international wire transfer services are usually provided in separate departments within a bank, documentation of incidents associated with these two services are kept in their respective departments, thus further decentralizing incident recordkeeping. For the most part, we depended on our key wire transfer contacts and their ability to recall incidents and to locate any documentation about the incidents. Thus, in contrast to the ATM incident data collection approach (which, because of the large number of incidents, required careful consideration of sampling-related issues), the wire transfer incident data collection was based on the banks providing whatever incident information they could.

In the following two subsections, we discuss issues related to the collection of incident and attitudinal data, respectively. Again, although a Summary Data Collection Instrument was developed (see Exhibit A.4), we do not discuss its use, as the data on total bank loss due to wire transfer fraud is, for the most part, not readily available.

Incident Data Collection

Wire transfer frauds, in addition to being infrequent, also tend to be unique. This is not the case in the ATM area, where there are a small number of incident types. The repetitive nature and large numbers of ATM incidents make it conducive to record them on a highly structured and detailed data collection instrument, like the one contained in Exhibit A.1. In contrast, wire transfer incidents, especially intentional fraudulent acts, are more conducive to a narrative description which could emphasize its unique aspects. Indeed, a bank's documentation of wire transfer incidents tends to be strictly in narrative form. Consequently, in developing the wire transfer incident data collection instrument, we were not able to benefit from the available Panel bank forms; instead, we relied on the advice of our wire transfer contacts.

Given the unique nature of wire transfer incidents, the Incident Data Collection Instrument we developed was necessarily less detailed than the ATM incident data collection instrument. The final version of the instrument -- shown in Exhibit A.3 -- is in six parts. Irrespective of the type of incident, all six parts should be completed. The six parts include:

A. Incident Characteristics. Incidents are first classified according to the scheme introduced in Section 1.2: intentional frauds (either successful or attempted) or inadventent errors (either leading to fraudulent absconding with funds or to an exposure without loss of funds). The type of incident captures the reason for the incident and details the nature of the fraud or error. Each of the incident types listed in Exhibit A.3, Question A.2 is depicted in Exhibit 1.10, which displays the potential vulnerabilities to fraud in a wire transfer system. The date of occurrence and the date of discovery are also requested, together with who discovered the incident.

B. Transaction Data. Transactions can be initiated in one of twelve ways, as indicated in Exhibit A.3, Question B.1. Other information requested about the wire transfer includes the origin and destination points, the primary wire transfer network involved and the purpose of the transaction (e.g., customer transfer, bank-to-bank transfer, advice to credit, etc.).

C. Reason For Incident. Reflecting the wide range of possible wire transfer incidents, 23 different incident causes are listed in Exhibit A.3, Question C.1. Who caused the incident is also requested.

D. Exposure/Loss Information. The exposure and loss information details the financial consequences of the incident. Inasmuch as every incident must result in some amount of exposure (i.e., potential loss) to the bank, this is recorded first. The amount of principal loss and any subsequent recovery are also requested.

E. Bank Action. This section of the instrument describes any personnel or procedural changes that the bank has made as a result of the incident.

F. General Comments. Additional space is provided for comments and other narrative information.

Copies of the instruments were distributed to our wire transfer contacts. At our initial site visits (i.e., in early 1984) the contacts were asked to complete an instrument for each incident that occurred within the preceeding five years. At our final site visits (i.e., in late 1984 and early 1985), we requested an instrument be completed for each incident that occurred in calender year 1984, as well as for any other incidents not previously supplied. In contrast to our ATM incident data collection approach in which we obtained copies of the incident forms and undertook their coding, we requested our wire transfer contacts to complete or code the incident forms because of two key considerations. First, banks are very reluctant to share their write-ups of sensitive wire transfer incidents; in fact, although we encouraged the banks to attach copies of any source documents, we received only a handful of such documents. Second, because of the rarity of wire transfer incidents, we felt that it would not be burdensome for our wire transfer contacts to do the coding. Actually, as detailed in Section 4.2, a total of 207 wire transfer incidents were coded. Did the fact that the banks themselves undertook the coding of the wire transfer incident compromise the consistency of the resultant database? We think not, as -- unlike the ATM Incident Data Collection Instrument -- the Wire Transfer Incident Data Collection Instrument is straightforward and easy to complete.

Finally, like the completed ATM incident instruments, the completed wire transfer incident instruments were keyed into a proprietary relational database management system, which was modified to reflect the unique characteristics of the Wire Transfer Incident Data Collection Instrument.

Attitudinal Data Collection

As noted earlier, losses due to wire transfer fraud are not readily segregated in the bank's financial reports. Thus, pertinent financial data was not available to estimate

the extent of wire transfer loss. Additionally, given the recognition that the Panel banks provided only a sample of wire transfer incidents, it was also not possible to use the incident-level data to make such an estimate. We were, however, able to gauge the bankers' attitude concerning wire transfer fraud and loss.

The 1983 Bank Administration Institute's (BAI's) Money Transfer Developments Conference provided a convenient attendance list of some 400 individuals, from which 155 wire transfer managers or related bank officials were identified (with at most one person per bank). The Attitudinal Data Collection Instrument in Exhibit A.5 was then mailed to each one of these 155 individuals: 73 (or 47.1 percent) of them responded. As detailed in Exhibit A.5, the Attitudinal Data Collection Instrument attempted to obtain the wire transfer managers' assessment of current and future causes of wire transfer fraud and loss, as well as their assessment of certain procedures for preventing wire transfer fraud and loss.

Again, the completed attitudinal instruments were keyed into a proprietary relational database management system for the purpose of analysis.

4.2 NATURE OF WIRE TRANSFER FRAUD

In all, we obtained 207 wire transfer incidents, with each one of our 16 Study Panel banks supplying at least one incident. Did this reflect the sum total of the Panel banks' experience with wire transfer fraud? Probably not. Because of difficulties with accessing the information and reluctance in sharing certain information, the banks, in essence, provided a sample of wire transfer incidents. Nevertheless, the sample does represent the single largest collection of data on wire transfer fraud and should serve to provide an adequate picture of the current nature of such fraud.

Our discussion of the nature of wire transfer fraud is in three parts. First, the incidents are described in terms of some background characteristics. Next, we discuss the disposition of the incident in regard to whether it is an error or a fraud. Finally, turning to an incident's dollar consequence, we address the incident's exposure and loss.

Incident Characteristics

Exhibit 4.1 contains a tabulation of the incident characteristics. Exhibit 4.1(a) shows that the 207 wire transfer incidents cover a period of approximately 6 years -- from 1979 to 1984. It should be noted that because of the small sample size, we do not analyze the wire transfer incidents on a year-by-year basis, as we do for the ATM incidents.

Exhibit 4.1(b) indicates that the incidents are most often customer transfers (45.6 percent of 180 incidents), followed by bank transfer in favor of a third bank (22.2 percent) and bank-to-bank transfers (13.9 percent). Can we interpret Exhibit 4.1(b) to imply that customer transfers constitute a severe problem -- that is, a problem which is disproportional to the overall number of

Exhibit 4.1

Wire Transfer: Incident Characteristics

Year	Column Percent (N=207)
1979 or earlier	7.3%
1980	12.1
1981	17.9
1982	16.9
1983	18.8
1984	27.0
TOTAL	100.0%

(a) Year of Occurrence

Category	Column Percent (N=180)
Customer Transfer	45.6%
Bank Transfer in Favor of 3rd Bank	22.2
Bank-to-Bank Transfer	13.9
Advice to Credit	7.2
Reverse Money Transfer	2.8
Other	8.3
TOTAL	100.0%

(b) Nature of Transaction

Exhibit 4.1

(Page 2 of 3)

Category	Column Percent (N=180)
Funds Transfer Network	32.3%
Telephone	28.9
Telex	23.3
Mail	3.3
Walk-In	3.3
Customer Terminal Link	3.3
Other	5.6
TOTAL	100.0%

(c) Method of Transaction Initiation

Network	Column Percent (N=148)
FedWire	66.9%
BankWire	12.2
SWIFT	10.8
CHIPS	5.4
Telex	4.7
TOTAL	100.0%

(d) Network Involved In Transaction

Exhibit 4.1

(Page 3 of 3)

Category	Column Percent (N=182)
Domestic	61.0%
International	39.0
TOTAL	100.0%

(e) Jurisdiction of Transaction

Category	Column Percent (N=181)
Central Wire Transfer Operation	33.1%
Sender	31.5
Receiver	13.3
Other Bank	11.6
Branch Bank	1.7
Other	8.8
TOTAL	100.0%

(f) Initiator or Discoverer of Incident

62

customer transfers? In order to answer this question, we would need to compare the incident distribution in Exhibit 4.1(b) with the corresponding distribution for all wire transfers. Unfortunately, the baseline data for all wire transfers is simply not readily available.

This interpretational problem applies to all the findings in Exhibit 4.1. Thus, we cannot say, as example, that in regard to the various methods of transaction initiation (see Exhibit 4.1(c)), the funds transfer network is involved in a disproportionate number of incidents; or that in regard to the various wire networks (see Exhibit 4.1(d)), that FedWire is involved in a disproportionate number of incidents; or that in regard to domestic and international wire transfers (see Exhibit 4.1(e)), the domestic transfers are involved in a disproportionate number of incidents. Nevertheless, Exhibit 4.1 does provide pertinent background information on the incidents.

One finding that is not affected by the interpretational problem is the fact that the wire transfer incidents are most often initiated or discovered by either personnel in the Central Wire Transfer Operation (33.1 percent of 181 incidents) or the sender (31.5 percent).

Errors and Frauds

Exhibit 4.2 indicates that the errors leading to loss or exposure (without loss), as opposed to intentional fraudulent acts, constitute the vast majority (194 out of 207) of the sample. This supports the hypothesis that although intentional fraudulent acts may be quite costly, they are rare; indeed, the 6 successful and 7 attempted fraudulent incidents in the study sample do not provide an adequate basis for any meaningful inferences to be made concerning such acts. However, as we noted in Section 1.2, frauds are not limited to intentional frauds. Indeed, 52.2 percent (108 of 207) of the incidents involved inadvertent errors that led to a fraud. These incidents typically result in the sudden and improper enrichment of an individual or a corporation. Errors leading to exposure without loss of principal constitute the second largest category of incidents in our study sample (i.e., 41.5 percent of the 207 incidents). However, this percentage is not indicative of their relative occurrence; indeed, it is the opinion of our Panel banks that such errors occur in some 0.2 to 0.5 percent of all wire transfers. Because several hundred of this type of errors are entered on their logs, the Panel banks decided against providing us with all of them. Consequently, our study sample is not representative of the universe of wire transfer incidents. However, as in the ATM incidents, while our distribution of the four categories of wire transfer incidents is not representative of the universe of wire transfer incidents, the incidents associated with any one of the four categories are representative of all incidents in that category (e.g., the 108 errors involving fraudulent absconding with funds are representative of all such errors).

Exhibit 4.2 also identifies the types of incidents (i.e., corresponding to the system vulnerabilities depicted in Exhibit 1.9) associated with each of the four incident categories. Although we hesitate to make conclusions regarding the fraudulent transfers because of the small sample size, it is noteworthy that 8 of the 13 successful and attempted fraudulent transfers involve the transfer being fraudulently initiated by a party external to the bank. The following attempted fraudulent transfer illustrates this type of incident. A person purporting to be authorized to call in wire transfers for a regular customer called the bank and initiated a transfer of $10,000. When the bank called back the customer to verify that he had in fact authorized the transfer, the customer stated that he knew nothing of the transfer. The wire transfer was immediately cancelled before it ever left the bank, and no loss was sustained. The failure to "call back" led to the successful commission of another fraudulent transfer, also externally initiated. In this case, Bank A, a small community bank, has a correspondent relationship with Bank B. Bank A received instructions from a person claiming to be a wire transfer operator at Bank B to effect a transfer of $100,000 to one of Bank A's accountholders. (In such a transfer, Bank B would credit the account that Bank A has with Bank B.) By indicating a sense of urgency, the recipient of the transfer managed to have the transfer paid out without having Bank A verify the transfer with Bank B. Failing to balance its financial statement with Bank B immediately, Bank A did not discover that its account with Bank B was not credited for five months. Informing Bank B of this fact, Bank A learned that Bank B had, in fact, never requested such a transfer. Bank A therefore sustained a loss of $100,000, one of the largest single-incident losses in our sample. Interestingly, attempts to externally initiate fraudulent wire transfers have been recently reported in the media [Ferris, 1985(b)]; they have involved con artists trying to initiate transfers by impersonating Federal Reserve employees.

As indicated in Exhibit 4.2, bank errors in message delivery is the dominant type of incident associated with inadvertent errors, both those leading to fraudulent absconding with funds and those leading to exposure without loss of principal. The following is a typical example of a bank error in message delivery leading to exposure without loss of principal. Bank A received an incoming message to credit Bank B with $50,000. By misinterpreting the abbreviated form of Bank B's name, Bank A inadvertently credited Bank C. Two weeks later, Bank B questioned Bank A about the transfer. Bank A then realized it had credited the wrong bank. After Bank C agreed to return the funds, Bank A then properly credited Bank B. Only interest-related loss was sustained by Bank A.

In terms of causes of wire transfer incidents, Exhibit 4.3 indicates that the errors are, for the most part, clerical in nature and committed by bank employees; they typically result in the duplication or the misrouting of messages (or payments), as illustrated by the following example. Bank A received a wire which they interpreted to contain instructions to credit a customer of

Exhibit 4.2

Wire Transfer: Incident Disposition by Type of Incident

Type of Incident	Incident Disposition by Column Percent			
	Successful Fraudulent Transfer (N=6)	Attempted Fraudulent Transfer (N=7)	Error Leading to Fraudulent Absconding (N=108)	Error Leading To Exposure Without Loss (N=86)
External Error in Message Initiation	0.0%	0.0%	1.2%	16.3%
Bank Error in Message Delivery	16.7	0.0	38.7	40.6
Bank Error in Message Content	0.0	0.0	12.0	16.3
Bank Error in Message Interpretation	0.0	0.0	2.4	3.5
Bank Error in Customer Notification	0.0	0.0	26.5	5.8
Bank Error in Accounting Entries	0.0	0.0	12.0	9.3
Failure to Follow Established Procedures	0.0	14.3	7.2	3.5
Transaction Fraudulently Entered (Internally)	16.7	14.3	0.0	0.0
Transaction Fraudulently Entered (Externally)	50.0	71.4	0.0	0.0
Transaction Altered in Processing	16.7	0.0	0.0	0.0
Fraudulent Destruction of Transaction Records	0.0	0.0	0.0	0.0
Other	0.0	0.0	0.0	4.7
TOTAL	100.0%	100.0%	100.0%	100.0%

Exhibit 4.3

Wire Transfer: Incident Disposition by Cause and Person Responsible

Incident Disposition by Column Percent

Category	Successful Fraudulent Transfer (N=6)	Attempted Fraudulent Transfer (N=7)	Error Leading To Fraudulent Absconding (N=108)	Error Leading To Exposure Without Loss (N=86)
Cause of Incident:				
Message Duplicated	0.0%	0.0%	57.5%	16.3%
Message Misrouted	0.0	0.0	8.3	31.5
Wrong Amount	16.7	0.0	12.0	7.0
Entry to Wrong Account	0.0	0.0	7.4	12.8
Wrong Currency	0.0	0.0	5.6	4.6
Collusion (External)	33.3	42.8	0.0	0.0
Collusion (Internal)	0.0	14.3	0.0	0.0
Insufficient Funds	0.0	14.3	0.0	5.8
Test Word Not Validated	0.0	0.0	0.9	1.2
Misuse of ID/Password	0.0	14.3	0.0	0.0
Data Line Compromise	0.0	0.0	0.0	1.2
Signature Forged	16.7	14.3	0.0	0.0
Message Altered	0.0	0.0	0.0	9.2
Uncollected Funds	0.0	0.0	0.9	0.0
Other	0.0	0.0	6.5	9.2
Unreported	33.3	0.0	0.9	1.2
TOTAL	100.0%	100.0%	100.0%	100.0%
Person Responsible For Incident:				
Bank Employee	66.7%	28.6%	96.3%	83.8%
Corporate Customer	0.0	0.0	0.0	7.0
Funds Transfer Network	0.0	0.0	0.9	2.3
Bank Computer System	0.0	0.0	0.0	2.3
Individual Customer	33.3	28.6	0.0	0.0
Unreported	0.0	42.8	2.8	4.6
TOTAL	100.0%	100.0%	100.0%	100.0%

Bank B with $20,000. Bank B informed Bank A that the true beneficiary was a customer of Bank C and not Bank B. (Correspondent Banks B and C are owned by the same holding company but, in fact, are independent banks.) Bank B advised Bank A that it would credit Bank C. A few days later, Bank A, not realizing that Bank B had properly completed the transfer, debited Bank B and credited Bank C. Thus, the beneficiary had been credited twice. Realizing their error, Bank A re-credited Bank B, but was unable to collect the $20,000 from the beneficiary, despite legal proceedings. Bank A thus sustained a loss of $20,000. Often, the beneficiary pockets all or part of the enrichment by physically absconding with the funds, by refusing to return them on the grounds that they were owed the funds by the sender, or by feigning ignorance and spending the funds. In these instances, an honest mistake -- which may be nothing more than a typographical error, a misplaced digit, or an error in considering, say, pesos as dollars -- makes possible the commission of a fraud -- perhaps, by a heretofore honest beneficiary. Even when the bank which stands to sustain the loss recovers all or the majority of the principal, there can be associated costs such as legal fees, interest and personnel time.

It should be noted that given the state of computer technology, the above cited clerical errors could be minimized. As examples, the computer could be programmed to alert wire transfer clerks when a message has been duplicated within, say, the last 24 hours. To minimize the risk of an error when transfers are initiated by telephone, the computer could print the dollar amount of the transfer in words on the screen and the clerk could then read the value to the customer for verification. For repetitive transfers, the computer could store in its memory partially completed data screens so that the clerk only needs to fill in the value of the transfer, hence minimizing the amount of data entry and, therefore, the risk of error. Additionally, the computer could map the network-specific codes into a common format so that the clerk only has to deal with a single format for all wire transfer networks. In sum, the computer should not only automate previous manual functions but also be programmed to assist in their execution. We also make this observation in Section 3.2, where we note that proper use of computer technology -- including immediate posting of all transactions and real-time hot carding -- could reduce ATM fraud.

A related issue is that automated systems require new procedures, different than those for the slower, labor-intensive manual systems. In fact, the renowned $10 million Rifkin heist was due to inadequate procedures or controls in the central wire transfer room. As an illustration, Exhibit 4.4 first identifies the current procedures that dominate the wire transfer area; it is strictly a one way flow of information with no effective checks and controls. The desired procedures depicted in the same exhibit add several "feed-back" steps to the current procedures; these steps stress both checks and controls. Although more cumbersome, the desired procedures would undoubtably reduce the incidence of both errors and frauds.

The above mentioned computer programs and desired procedures would certainly have prevented the majority of incidents in our study sample. Yet, it is interesting to note that banks today seem to be more concerned about developing procedures to guard against the type of fruadulent incidents not present in our study sample, namely those dealing with electronic attacks on the computer or the telecommunications system, as well as other "technologically sophisticated" frauds [Misra, 1984]. At the Federal level, the Treasury Department recently issued a directive requiring all Federal electronic fund transfers to be "authenticated or electronically sealed" [Government Data Systems, 1985]. The financial community is clearly fearful that the public's increasing computer literacy will render wire transfer systems more vulnerable to technologically sophisticated fraud. This observation is supported by our attitudinal survey, as detailed in Section 4.3.

Exposure and Loss

As summarized in Exhibit 4.5, the 175 wire transfer incidents for which there were exposure information resulted in an average bank exposure per incident of $942,450 with a maximum of over $37 million. This average is somewhat misleading since, as pointed out in Exhibit 4.6, the average exposure in recent years has been approximately $1.6 million, which is lower than the 2.3 million average FedWire transaction amount indicated in Exhibit 1.6.

Returning to Exhibit 4.5, a surprising statistic is that the average exposure for those incidents with no bank loss is 59.1 times that for incidents with some bank loss; while it might be expected that in incidents with large exposures the bank would make every effort to recover the funds, the 59.1 factor is significant. Indeed, the size of this factor might lead one to conjecture that incidents with large exposures and subsequent losses -- although undoubtedly few -- were not provided to the study. Interestingly, a similar difference in exposure amounts exists between domestic and international incidents, with the average domestic exposure being 41.5 times greater than the average international exposure.

As defined earlier in Section 3.2 for ATM incidents, the exposure time in wire transfer incidents is equal to the total elapsed time between the date of incident occurrence and the date the bank is notified or becomes aware of the incident. As is the case with ATM incidents, a reasonable hypothesis is that the longer the exposure, the greater the expected loss. This hypothesis is confirmed by the figures in Exhibit 4.5 where incidents with some loss had an average exposure time of 158 days, which was 4.8 times longer than the average exposure time for incidents with no loss. When analyzed by jurisdiction, however, the hypothesis is not supported since, international incidents, while being exposed 2.8 times longer than their domestic counterparts, experienced an average net -- following recovery -- loss of $12,429, a figure 57.5 percent less than that of domestic transfers (see Exhibit 4.7).

Exhibit 4:4

Wire Transfer: Current and Desired Procedures

Current Procedures

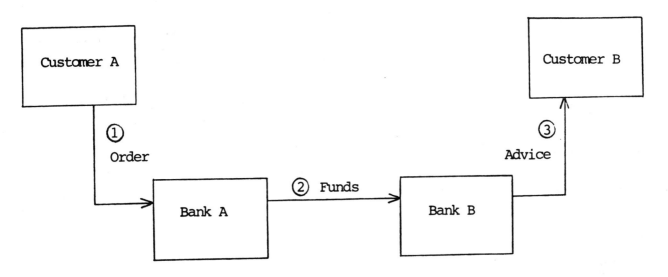

Desired Procedures

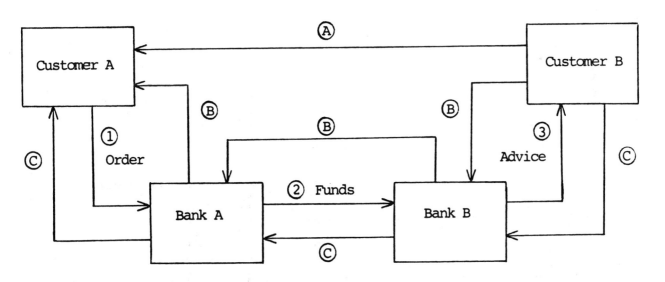

A: Invoice;   B: Request For Pay;   C: Receipt

Exhibit 4.6

Wire Transfer: Average Bank Exposure by Year of Incident Occurrence

Year of Occurrence	Number	Average Exposure
1979 or before	15	$ 33,726
1980	25	30,127
1981	37	128,780
1982	34	1,756,624
1983	33	1,606,444
1984	31	1,489,252

Exhibit 4.7

Wire Transfer: Bank Losses by Recovery Disposition and Jurisdiction

Category	Wire Transfer Incidents		Net Bank Loss		
	Number	Column %	Minimum	Average	Maximum
Recovery Disposition:					
Some Recovery	30	33.0%	$ 0	$16,145	$279,933
No Recovery	61	67.0	$30	$17,111	$200,000
Jurisdiction:					
Domestic	41	45.1%	$ 0	$21,611	$279,933
International	50	54.9	$ 0	$12,429	$200,000
All Loss Incidents	91	100.0%	$ 0	$16,793	$279,933

Exhibit 4.7 summarizes the wire transfer losses in the 91 incidents in which the bank sustained a loss. The average net loss in these incidents is $16,793. One might think that, given wire transfer incidents are rare, bankers would not be overly concerned with the $16,793 figure. Indeed, the key issue in this EFT technology is not so much actual loss experience -- even though the maximum incident loss in our study sample was $279,933, a sizable figure under any circumstances -- but potential losses, which as shown in Exhibit 4.6, could have averaged $1.6 million per incident during the past three years. This, more than anything else, instills fear in the bankers.

4.3   ATTITUDES TOWARD WIRE TRANSFER FRAUD

As indicated in Section 4.1, we mailed a questionaire (i.e., the Attitudinal Data Collection Instrument contained in Exhibit A.5) to 155 attendees of the 1983 BAI Money Transfer Developments Conference. We received 73 (i.e., 47.1 percent of 155) completed questionaires -- an excellent response rate. Of the 73 respondents, 78.1 percent were wire transfer managers, and, surprisingly, 47.9 percent identified themselves and indicated a willingness to provide incident-level data. This further encourages one to believe that consistent and accurate data on wire transfer fraud and loss can be collected.

In the remainder of this section, we consider certain characteristics of the respondents, their attitude concerning the causes of wire transfer fraud and loss, and their fear of fraud and loss, followed by a review of the reactions to our survey findings.

Respondent Characteristics

Looking more closely at the characteristics of the responding banks, Exhibit 4.8 describes them in terms of their wire transfer volume, value and losses. That these are major financial institutions is borne out by the average of 2,072 wire transfers per day, although this figure is somewhat less than the Panel bank's average of 3,343 transfers per day, as reported in Section 2.3. In terms of dollar volume, the respondents average $7.6 billion per day, ranging as high as $110 billion.

In light of the incidents reported by our Panel banks, the average annual loss of $23,327 estimated by the respondents is not surprising; given an average loss per incident of $16,793 (see Exhibit 4.7), this translates to 1.4 loss incidents per year per bank that reported a loss. Nevertheless, despite the absolute sizes of the current and projected losses, it is important to observe that the banks are projecting a significant 69.5 percent increase in their annual losses in 5 years. This finding supports the observation made in Section 4.2 that there exists a high level of fear of fraud and loss among members of the wire transfer community.

Causes of Fraud and Loss

When asked to identify the current and future causes of wire transfer fraud and loss,

the respondents gave the answers summarized in Exhibit 4.9. As with the incidents reported by the Study Panel banks, duplicated messages and related errors figure prominently in their responses. While these causes are projected to remain fairly constant -- albeit at a high level -- in 5 years, the more technical causes such as message alteration, password and test key compromising, and database alterations are projected to increase substantially. One can conclude from these findings that the banks are expecting an increase in the level of wire transfer fraud and loss, as well as an increase in the sophistication with which the fraud is perpetrated.

Fear of Fraud and Loss

In conversations with wire transfer managers and bank officials, we detect considerable concern or fear about being hit with large wire tranfer losses, even though their own banks might not yet have experienced one. The question arises as to whether their fears would be any different if they had experienced at least one wire transfer loss versus not having had any such experience. Surprisingly, Exhibit 4.10 shows that those with no loss experience are more than twice as concerned about the contribution the stated causes would make to wire transfer fraud and loss than those with loss experience. Consequently, the current fear among wire transfer managers and bank officials is greater than warranted, according to those who have experienced wire transfer loss. This is certainly a revealing finding; it should provide comfort to the banking industry. Indeed, based on the results documented in Section 4.3, the banking industry should be as concerned about ATM fraud as it seems to be about wire transfer fraud.

Reaction to Survey Findings

As noted in Section 2.2, we presented the findings of our attitudinal survey -- together with our wire trasnfer incident data analysis -- at the 1984 BAI Money Transfer Development Conference. Being the first presentation ever to focus on fraud-related statistics, it was one of the best attended sessions at the Conference. The BAI was pleased with both the turnout and the substance of the report, and the daily financial newspaper American Banker was sufficiently impressed so as to run the Ferris [1984] article of the presentation as a cover-page story. The attendees were quite impressed and expressed agreement with our findings, in particular our finding that the fear of wire transfer fraud is greater than actual losses would warrent.

As a result of the presentation, several attendees volunteered to provide data on their wire transfer incidents. Additionally, many attendees asked to be put on the mailing list for the final study report.

Exhibit 4.8

Wire Transfer: Survey Findings by Bank Background and Loss Estimates

Category	Number of Respondents	Low Figure	Average Figure	High Figure
Bank Background:				
Daily Number of Transfers per Bank	72	50	2,072	30,000
Daily Dollar Volume of Transfers per Bank	69	$800,000	$7.6 billion	$110.0 billion
Loss Estimates:				
Current Annual Loss per Bank (That Sustained a Loss)	35	$100	$23,327	$215,000
Annual Loss per Bank (That Expects a Loss) 5 Years From Now	28	$100	$39,548	$500,000

Exhibit 4.5

Wire Transfer: Bank Exposure and Days of Exposure by Loss Disposition and Jurisdiction

| Category | Wire Transfer Incidents | | Bank Exposure | | | Average Number of Days of Exposure |
	Number	Column %	Minimum	Average	Maximum	
Loss Disposition:						
Some Bank Loss	91	52.0%	$30	$ 32,600	$ 315,000	158
No Bank Loss	84	48.0	$30	$1,928,120	$37,357,000	33
Jurisdiction:						
Domestic Incident	106	60.6%	$30	$1,531,705	$37,357,000	57
International Incident	69	39.4	$30	$ 37,216	$ 380,000	161
All Incidents	175	100.0%	$30	$ 942,450	$37,357,000	98

68

Exhibit 4.9

Wire Transfer: Survey Findings by Causes of Current and Expected Fraud and Loss

Cause	Number of Respondents	Percent of Respondents Indicating That The Stated Cause:	
		"Currently Contributes to Fraud and Loss"	"Will in 5 Years Contribute to Fraud and Loss"*
Call-Back Failure	45	53.3%	71.1%
Collusion (Internal)	38	28.9%	55.3%
Collusion (External)	37	37.8%	59.5%
Data Line Compromise	39	25.6%	43.6%
Entry Posted to Wrong Account	50	84.0%	86.0%
Insufficient Funds	45	53.3%	53.3%
Message Altered	42	26.2%	40.5%
Message Duplicated	46	80.4%	71.7%
Misuse of Password	44	29.5%	38.6%
Payment Without Proper I.D.	41	41.5%	48.8%
PIN Compromised	36	25.0%	36.1%
Test Key Compromised	41	17.1%	39.0%
Unauthorized Access to Operations Area	46	19.6%	26.1%
Unauthorized Alteration of Database	36	22.2%	41.7%
OVERALL	—	38.9%	50.8%

* Assuming no new fraud prevention measures are adopted in the interim.

73

Exhibit 4.10

Wire Transfer: Survey Findings by Current Loss Experience

Cause	Banks With Current Loss		Banks With No Current Loss	
	Number of Respondents	Percent of Respondents Indicating that the Stated Cause "Currently Contributes to Fraud and Loss"	Number of Respondents	Percent of Respondents Indicating that the Stated Cause "Currently Contributes to Fraud and Loss"
Call-Back Failure	30	33.3%	22	72.7%
Collusion (Internal)	28	7.1%	20	50.0%
Collusion (External)	29	31.0%	17	58.8%
Data Line Compromise	28	0.0%	21	47.6%
Entry Passed to Wrong Account	32	87.5%	22	72.7%
Insufficient Funds	29	51.7%	22	50.0%
Message Altered	30	6.7%	21	47.6%
Message Duplicated	32	71.9%	22	68.2%
Misuse of Password	30	16.7%	22	50.0%
Payment Without Proper I.D.	29	20.7%	21	57.1%
PIN Compromised	27	3.7%	20	45.0%
Test Key Compromised	30	6.7%	18	33.3%
Unauthorized Access to Operations Area	30	3.3%	22	36.4%
Unauthorized Alteration of Database	28	3.6%	22	36.4%
OVERALL	—	24.6%	—	51.8%

5 CONCLUSION

A summary of the major study results, a modeling of EFT fraud from a risk perspective, and a discussion of future research efforts are contained in Sections 5.1 through 5.3, respectively.

5.1 SUMMARY

This report documents a pilot effort at assessing the nature and extent of electronic fund transfer (EFT) fraud. Prior to this effort, the available information has been limited to newspaper accounts of celebrated incidents or analyses of questionaire surveys with low returns. The effort is based on an alternative approach of obtaining valid and consistent fraud data -- directly from a panel of banks. With the support of the Association of Reserve City Bankers (ARCB), we were able to convene a Study Panel of 16 banks, from whom we obtained incident and summary fraud data on two of the most widely used EFT technologies -- automated teller machine (ATM) and wire transfer.

The results of this effort have demonstrated first and foremost that the Panel approach is viable. The willingness of the banking community to participate in the effort and the enthusiasm generated by the resultant findings are evidenced by the following events:

- An unexpectedly high percentage of the invited banks chose to participate in the study. We had originally invited 18 banks to participate, hoping that 12 would accept. In the end, 16 banks accepted our invitation.

- The Study Panel banks have provided over 4,000 ATM incidents and over 200 wire transfer incidents, as well as important summary data on ATM fraud and loss.

- Nearly half of the respondents to an attitudinal survey of wire transfer managers have indicated their willingness to participate in future fraud-related data collection efforts.

- The two study-related Special Reports published by the Bureau of Justice Statistics (BJS) have received coast-to-coast radio, newspaper, and television coverage.

- The banking community has expressed great interest in this study, as evidenced by our well-received presentations at conferences sponsored by the Bank Administration Institute (BAI) and the American Bankers Association (ABA).

Before summarizing the key study findings, we should reiterate that this has been a pilot study and all findings should be regarded as preliminary. Obviously, a 16-bank panel cannot be representative of the more than 14,000 commercial banks in the U.S. Moreover, the Panel banks are all ARCB-member banks, each with assets of over $1 billion.

In regard to ATM fraud, the key findings are:

- In 1983, it is estimated that there were 2.7 billion ATM transactions (i.e., withdrawals or deposits) involving $262 billion. Activity increased in 1984 to 3.0 billion transactions, resulting in a dollar volume of $291 billion.

- Because of the requirement of Federal Regulation E (Reg E), detailed fraud-related information is available at banks for those ATM incidents involving an accountholder complaint. Less complete records are maintained on incidents involving only bank complaints.

- The Panel banks supplied 2,707 1983 and 1,480 1984 ATM incidents, 42 percent of which were determined to be potentially fraudulent, involving, as examples, unauthorized use of lost or stolen cards, overdrafts, and "bad" deposits.

- In most respects, the 1984 ATM incidents are comparable to those for 1983; any differences cannot be interpreted as a trend but could most likely be accounted for by the year-to-year variation in the underlying statistic.

- Lost or stolen cards are the leading cause of ATM fraud and bank losses. Present in many of these incidents is accountholder negligence, which, partially because of Reg E requirements, is contributing to bank losses.

- Banks could reduce ATM fraud by effectively utilizing computer technology when designing their ATM systems.

- Bank losses per incident are small (roughly $200 per incident), but scam-related incidents in the study sample underscore the potential for large single-incident losses (in the thousands of dollars).

- The annual nationwide bank loss due to ATM fraud is estimated at between $70 and $100 million. On a per transaction and dollar volume basis, ATM fraud losses are significantly lower than credit card fraud losses.

In regard to wire transfer fraud, the key findings are:

- In 1984, roughly $668 billion per day was transferred over the FedWire and CHIPS networks alone, representing a 48 percent increase since 1980.

- Data collection in the wire transfer area was more difficult than in the ATM area, primarily because wire transfer frauds are rare and there is no formal mechanism -- like Reg E -- for documenting them. As a result, the extent of wire transfer fraud could not be estimated, as summary data on wire transfer fraud and loss could not be readily obtained.

- A total of 207 wire transfer incidents occurring in the past six years were obtained from the Panel banks. Not surprisingly, the vast majority of the incidents are errors leading to either fraudulent absconding with funds or exposure without loss of principal, as opposed to intentional fraudulent acts.

- As in the ATM area, computers could be used more effectively to prevent wire transfer fraud, especially those resulting from clerical errors.

- The exposure (i.e., potential loss) per wire transfer incident averaged $942,450. However, if one considers only those incidents occurring within the past three years, the average exposure would be $1.6 million.

- Wire transfer managers are projecting a significant increase in their annual fraud losses in the next five years, thus supporting the observation that there exists a high level of fear of fraud in the wire transfer community.

- According to wire transfer managers who have experienced wire transfer frauds, the current fear of fraud is greater than warranted. Indeed, the banking industry should be as concerned about ATM fraud as it seems to be about wire transfer fraud.

Finally, the detailed data collection instruments which have been used in this pilot effort have been developed to (i) facilitate data collection, coding and analysis; (ii) be straightforwardly adopted in an operational environment (so that they could be used by the banks for administrative and investigative purposes); and (iii) be easily implemented on a computer (as we did for analysis purposes). Future efforts to collect EFT fraud data can obviously benefit from these instruments.

In conclusion, it should again be stated that in addition to providing insight on the nature and extent of EFT fraud, this pilot effort has shown that valid and consistent data can be obtained directly from banks and that a larger panel, one that can provide an on-going source of information on EFT fraud, could and should be established.

5.2 RISK MODELING

The content of this section should be regarded as preliminary and developmental in nature. It reflects the results of a self-imposed task that grew out of our review of EFT security controls and procedures at the Panel banks. More specifically, we noted that the system of controls and procedures vary widely from bank to bank, with each system having its own particular strengths and weaknesses. The question arises as to which system is "better" -- that is, which system has the lowest risk-to-fraud. Consequently, building on a previous effort [Tien and Cahn, 1983], we sought to develop a sound analytical framework to model the risk-to-fraud of EFT systems. Such a framework would allow different systems to be compared and hypothetical systems to be evaluated.

The remainder of this section consists of three parts: the risk model, the risk measurement process, and an example risk analysis.

Risk Model

In addressing the concept of risk within the general context of EFT fraud prevention, it is helpful to identify a specific context, even though the discussion is applicable to any EFT fraud prevention context. Inasmuch as our data is more complete in the ATM area than in the wire trasnfer area, it is appropriate to focus on the ATM fraud prevention problem -- in particular, the unauthorized use of a lost or stolen card, which is the leading cause of ATM fraud.

The risk model developed herein is based on the recognition that an EFT fraud (in this case, an unauthorized use of a missing card) can be prevented or mitigated at three possible points during the commission of the fraud. First, the fraud attempt may not even be made if, for example, the would-be erpetrator realizes that his or her chance of being apprehended outweighs his or her potential gain from the fraud. Thus, having all ATMs on the bank's premise or equipping the ATMs with cameras might serve to deter a fraud attempt. Second, even if a fraud attempt is made, it is possible that the perpetrator may not be able to gain access to the account because of, for example, a "front-end" security measure (e.g., PINs). Third, even if the perpetrator gains access to the account, it is yet possible that an "on-line" security measure (e.g., a daily withdrawal limit) could minimize the adverse financial consequences.

The above three steps of a fraud commission can be measured by the following three variables, respectively:

(i) Likelihood [L(n)]: probability that n fraud attempts are made in, say, a one year period.

(ii) Vulnerability [V]: probability that, given a fraud attempt, the attempt is successful.

(iii) Cost [C]: cost or loss, given that a fraud attempt is successful.

76

Mathematically, it can be shown that the expected number of attempted frauds per year is equal to:

$$E[\text{Attempted Frauds}] = \sum_{n=0}^{\infty} nL(n) \qquad (5.1)$$

Similarly, the expected number of successful fraud attempts per year is equal to:

$$E[\text{Sucessful Frauds}] = \sum_{n=0}^{\infty} nL(n)V \qquad (5.2)$$

The risk-to-fraud -- R -- can then be defined as the expected cost or loss due to all successful frauds per year, and it can be shown to be equal to:

$$R = E[\text{Fraud-Related Cost}] = \sum_{n=0}^{\infty} nL(n)VC \qquad (5.3)$$

In sum, a fraud prevention system would attempt to minimize the risk-to-fraud by implementing measures which would decrease either L, or V, or C, or any combination of the three: for example, effective hot carding procedures might impact all three risk components.

Although intuitively satisfying, the model represented by (5.3) is actually a simple version of perhaps a more complex -- and, hopefully, more realistic -- model. For example, the model assumes that the vulnerability of a bank to any fraud attempt is the same. However, it might be more realistic to assume that there is a "learning process" so that the bank becomes less vulnerable with each attempted fraud: in such a case, V would be a function of n, the number of fraud attempts per year. Similarly, C could also be a function of n. Another level of complexity might be the potential interaction between the variables L, V, and C. Yet, irrespective of how simple or unreal the model represented by (5.3) might be, it still does provide at least an initial framework for evaluating the security of an EFT system.

Risk Measurement

While the risk model represented by (5.3) may be mathematically simple and straightforward, applying the model was more difficult. First, we had to identify the specific measures which can impact each of the risk components. These measures are listed in Exhibit 5.1 in the context of a risk assessment instrument. It should be noted that inasmuch as this exercise is for illustrative purposes, we do not claim that the list is complete. Second, it was necessary to provide a measurement scale for each of the risk components and their associated measures. Even though likelihood and vulnerability, as defined above, are probabilistic concepts (and therefore, by convention, measured on a continuous scale between 0 and 1), we decided to employ a discrete scale from 1 to 5, for both likelihood and vulnerability, so as to facilitate the implementation of the instruments. (A 1 indicates very low likelihood/vulnerability, while a 5 indicates very high likelihood/vulnerability.) A 1 to 5 scale was also employed for the cost measure. Obviously, the scoring of the likelihood, vulnerability, and cost measures in Exhibit 5.1 are, to a large degree, subjective: again, they are indicated for illustrative purposes.

For example, as shown in Exhibit 5.1, a customer-selected PIN selection strategy is scored lower (i.e., is viewed as less vulnerable) than a bank-assigned PIN selection strategy. One could certainly argue this scoring, but, as discussed in Section 3.2, our data is inconclusive on this subject. Third, while our risk model is based on obtaining the likelihood of n fraud attempts per year (for $n=1,2,...\infty$), we had to limit the likelihood assessment to that of a single fraud attempt, inasmuch as the assessment of a distribution of probabilities would have been overwhelming, especially given the preliminary nature of our investigation.

Using the information we gathered informally through conversations with our ATM bank contacts, we were able to apply the risk model to two Panel banks: their respective scores are indicated in italics in Exhibit 5.1.

Risk Analysis

After completing the ATM Risk Assessment Instrument for the two Panel banks, we had to decide how to aggregate the individual measure scores within each of the three risk components or categories in order to obtain an overall risk score. One possibility was to take the arithmetic average of all the scores, which, by implication, means equally weighting all the associated measures. Another possibility was to apply different weights to each of the measures. For example, in the cost category, perhaps the "withdrawal limit per day" measure should be given a higher weight than the "number of transactions allowed per day" measure. A third possibility was based on a "weakest link" approach, whereby the value assigned to each of the three categories is the maximum of the values within that particular category. In the end, given the preliminary nature of our analysis, we decided to employ the simple arithmetic averaging scheme. Additionally, for convenience, we converted the 1-5 scale for L, V, and C into a 0-1 scale for L (i.e., 1 corresponds to 0.00, 2 corresponds to 0.25, 3 corresponds to 0.50, 4 corresponds to 0.75, 5 corresponds to 1.00), a 0-1 scale for V, and a 0-100 scale for C (i.e., 1 corresponds to 0, 2 corresponds to 25, 3 corresponds to 50, 4 corresponds to 75, 5 corresponds to 100): consequently, R, the risk-to-fraud measure, is also on a 0-100 scale, as it is the product of L, V, and C.

Based on the scores contained in Exhibit 5.1, the resultant -- arithmetically averaged -- risk-to-fraud statistics are presented in Exhibit 5.2. (For example, Bank A's Vulnerability scores in Exhibit 5.1, Questions 2.1, 2.2, and 2.3 are 3, 2, and 1, respectively. The average of these three numbers is 2.0, which converts to 0.25 on the 0-1 scale, as indicated by the conversion factors listed above.) Notice that Bank A has a lower score than Bank B in each one of the three categories: consequently, it has a lower overall risk-to-fraud score. Indeed, Bank A's ATM fraud loss ratios (i.e., loss per transaction and loss per dollar volume) are lower than those for Bank B. While a lack of data precluded a risk assessment of all the Panel banks, it is unlikely that any of the Panel banks would have a large risk-to-fraud

Exhibit 5.1

ATM: Risk Assessment Instrument

Bank: Bank A/Bank B

1 LIKELIHOOD OF ATTEMPT TO USE MISSING CARD

1.1 Bank Distribution System of Cards and PINs

1/3

1 = Customer picks up card and PIN at bank

3 = Card and PIN mailed separately

5 = Card and PIN mailed together

1.2 Location of ATMs; Lighting

3/2

1 = All ATMs on bank premise

5 = All ATMs off bank premise with poor lighting

1.3 Cameras

5/5

1 = 80-100 percent of ATMs camera-equipped
2 = 60-79 percent of ATMs camera-equipped
3 = 40-59 percent of ATMs camera-equipped
4 = 20-39 percent of ATMs camera-equipped
5 = 0-19 percent of ATMs camera-equipped

2 VULNERABILITY THAT UNAUTHORIZED USER GAINS ACCESS TO ATM SYSTEM

2.1 Hot Carding

3/1

1 = 24-hour on-line hot carding

5 = Business hour batch hot carding only

Exhibit 5.1

(page 2 of 3)

2.2 Number of Incorrect PIN tries allowed

2/2

1 = < 4

5 = unlimited

2.3 PIN Selection Scheme

1/4

1 = Customer—selected; PIN unknown to bank personnel

5 = Bank-assigned random number; PIN known to bank personnel

3 COST OF SUCCESSFUL ENTRY INTO ATM SYSTEM

3.1 Withdrawal Limit per Day

1/3

1 = $200 or less

5 = unlimited

3.2 Number of Transactions Allowed Per Day

2/2

1 = < 4

5 = unlimited

Exhibit 5.1

(page 3 of 3)

3.3 Provisional Credit for Deposits

4/4

1 = Account not credited until check clears

5 = Account credited at time of deposit

3.4 Off-Line Policy

1/3

1 = No off-line operation

3 = Off-line operation with controls

5 = Off-line operation without controls

3.5 Hot Carding

3/1

1 = 24-hour on-line hot carding

5 = Business hour batch hot carding only

3.6 Ticklers

3/3

1 = Generate fraud suspect list daily

5 = No monitoring of suspicious card activity

Exhibit 5.2

ATM: Risk-to-Fraud Statistics

Bank	Scores Based On Arithmetic Average of Entries in Exhibit 5.1			
	Likelihood	Vulnerability	Cost	Risk
Bank A	0.50	0.25	33.3	4.2
Bank B	0.58	0.33	41.7	8.0

score; their scores would most likely be between 4.2 and 8.0 (i.e., the risk-to-fraud scores of Banks A and B, respectively).

As mentioned earlier in this section, this model could certainly be made more complex. Additionally, the risk-to-fraud framework could be applied to other EFT fraud prevention settings, including wire transfer fraud, where one could examine the likelihood a fraudulent wire transfer is attempted, the probability (i.e., vulnerability) the transfer is completed (including the probability of the money being successfully withdrawn from the banking system), and the cost of such a fraud. This is, of course, a possible area for future study, as are other areas considered in the following section.

5.3 FUTURE EFFORTS

While the findings of this study have been significant, there remain many areas to explore that can extend our knowledge of EFT fraud. One possible area, namely an attempt to systematically assess the risk-to-fraud in an EFT system, is proposed in Section 5.2. Several additional areas are briefly outlined below, each of which builds on and extends the results in this pilot effort. In terms of timing, it should be noted that each of the below efforts should be carried out for at least a two year period.

-   Study Panel: Nature of ATM and Wire Transfer Fraud. To gain better knowledge, as well as important trend information, about the nature of ATM and wire transfer fraud, incident data should be obtained from the current Study Panel of 16 banks. This would involve continued use of the ATM and wire transfer incident data collection instruments.

-   Study Panel: Extent of Wire Transfer Fraud. As indicated throughout Section 4, summary data on wire transfer fraud and loss is not readily available. In this effort, it is proposed that extensive work be undertaken jointly with the Study Panel banks to first establish a simple but consistent procedure for gathering summary data -- on wire transfer fraud and loss, as well as overall wire transfer volume -- on an on-going basis. Following implementation of the procedure, annual summary data should be obtained so that a preliminary estimate of the extent of wire transfer fraud could be determined.

-   National Panel: Extent of ATM Fraud. In addition to reconvening the original Study Panel, another possible future effort would be to establish a large panel of perhaps 100 financial institutions, including institutions other than commercial banks (e.g., mutual savings banks and savings and loan associations). Potential members of this National Panel could be drawn from the ARCB membership, or from

the ABA membership (which has expressed an interest in expanding this pilot effort) or through a less formal mechanism. The larger National Panel would allow for a more statistically significant estimate of the extent of ATM fraud than the current Study Panel.

-   National Panel: Nature and Extent of Wire Transfer Fraud. Inasmuch as wire transfer incidents are rare, the large National Panel could provide a sample of incidents that could be large enough to yield statistically significant results. Also, based on the data gathering procedure to be established in an above Study Panel effort, the National Panel could be requested to furnish summary wire transfer data, upon which a statistically significant estimate of the extent of wire transfer fraud could be made.

-   ATM Regional Networks: Nature and Extent of ATM Fraud. This effort involves contacting several ATM regional networks and obtaining fraud-related data from a systems perspective. Contacts with these networks could be made through the courtesy of some of the Study Panel banks which belong to such networks. As mentioned in Section 1.1, the number and importance of ATM networks has increased rapidly in the past five years. Several factors have provided impetus for a financial institution to form or join an ATM network, including lowering the cost of providing ATM services, providing more convenient services to its cardholders, and avoiding prohibitions against interstate banking. Also, smaller financial institutions, which could not afford the large initial costs of building their own ATM system, can now join an ATM network. The character of ATM fraud in a network environment should be investigated, including obtaining answers to such questions as: What security requirements are mandated of member banks of a network? In case of a fraud occurrence, what is the responsibility of the "host" bank which owns the ATM through which the fraud is committed? Likewise, what is the resonsibility of the "switch" which owns or operates the network? Also, what is the responsibility of the "home" bank against which a fraud is committed? What are related legal issues (see, for example, Polmer and Epperson [1981])?

-   Wire Transfer Networks: Nature and Extent of Wire Transfer Fraud. Similar to the approach discussed above concerning ATM Regional Networks, this effort involves contacting one or more of the four primary wire transfer networks (see Section 1.1), discussing our wire transfer findings with them, and then obtaining some fraud-related system data. Possible areas to investigate include: What security requirements are mandated of member banks of a network? In case of a fraud occurrence, what is the responsibility of the "sender" bank which initiates the wire transfer? Likewise, what is the responsibility of the owner or operator of the network? Also, what is the responsibility of the "receiving" bank which receives the wire transfer? What are related legal issues?

POS Panel: Nature and Extent of POS Fraud. As discussed in Section 1.1, point-of-sale (POS) systems are on the verge of becoming a dominant force in the Nation's payment system. In addition, as suggested in Exhibit 5.3, a full-scale POS system is actually a combination of the credit card and ATM systems, inasmuch as POS involves both retail purchases and immediate funds transfer between accountholder accounts. As such, POS would probably inherit the fraud-related problems of both these systems. The approach to assessing the nature and extent of POS fraud could be similar to the approach we have taken in the ATM and wire transfer areas. Study Panel banks and other financial institutions having extensive POS experience could be asked to join a POS Panel. In particular, as we have done in the ATM and wire transfer areas, both incident-level and summary-level POS data should be obtained from the POS Panel banks. Also, operationally-oriented POS data collection instruments -- which could be easily implemented on a computer --should be developed.

Permanent National Panel: Institutionalization of EFT Fraud Measurement. It is obvious that specially-tailored studies on EFT fraud cannot continue to be undertaken indefinitely. What is needed is an on-going mechanism for assessing or measuring the nature and extent of EFT fraud -- in particular, in the ATM, wire transfer and POS areas. To this end, we propose that the National Panel be maintained on a permanent basis, and financial institutions rotate through the Panel on, say, a five-year basis (i.e., every year, 20 percent of the Panel would be replaced). This Permanent National Panel would have to be housed in a national banking organization, which would be responsible for undertaking the analysis of the fraud data provided by the Panel banks. Certainly, the data collection instruments and procedures developed in this pilot effort should help in the proposed institutionalization effort. Indeed, the Permanent National Panel would accomplish what

our study has taken a first step toward: providing a formal mechanism to measure EFT fraud on an on-going basis.

Exhibit 5.3

POS: As Compared With Credit Card and ATM

Features	Credit Card	Automatic Teller Machine (ATM)	Point-Of Sale (POS)
• Access Mechanism	• Credit Card/ Signature	• ATM Card/PIN	• ATM Card/PIN
• Credit Card Authorization	• By phone, for purchases above a specified amount.		• By terminal, for purchases above a certain amount.
• National Negative File	• Requires timely update.		• Requires timely update.
• Charge-Back or Refund	• Posted on next monthly bill.		• Requires immediate posting in customer's account.
• Cash Withdrawal		• Limited to a prespecified amount per day.	• Permitted only through purchases.
• Check Deposit		• Permitted.	
• Balance Inquiry		• Permitted.	
• Funds Transfer/ Direct Debit		• Permitted between customer's own accounts.	• Permitted between customer and merchant accounts.
• Hot Carding		• Requires timely update.	• Requires timely update.
• Check Authorization			• Permitted.

REFERENCES

American Banker. "Robbery Victims at ATMs in Texas Denied Reimbursement by Banks", 24 May 1984.

American Bankers Association. "ATM Cameras Help Cut 'Family' Fraud". ABA Banking Journal, May 1983.

American Bar Association (Task Force on Computer Crime). Report On Computer Crime. Washington, D.C.: author, 1984.

American Institute of Certified Public Accountants. Report on the Study of EDP-Related Fraud in the Banking and Insurance Industries. New York: author, 1984.

Arthur D. Little, Inc. Issues and Needs in the Nation's Payment System. Cambridge, Mass.: author, 1982.

Association of Reserve City Bankers. Risks in the Electronic Payment Systems: Report of the Risk Task Force. Washington, D.C.: author, 1983.

Bank Administration Institute. 1984 EFT Survey. Forthcoming report, 1985.

Bank Network News. "EFT Data Book", 1984.

Bank Network News. "Regional Networks Take a POS Plunge". 11 January 1985.

Bergen, M. "Broader Card Base, Lower Costs Spur Banks to Offer POS in '84". Bank Systems and Equipment, August 1984.

Boyle, W.M. ATM Security. Rolling Meadows, Illinois: Bank Administration Institute, 1983.

Colton, K.W., Tien, J.M., Tvedt, S., and Barnett, A.I. (Public Systems Evaluation, Inc., Cambridge, Mass.). Computer Crime: Electronic Fund Transfer Systems and Crime. Washington, D.C.: Bureau of Justice Statistics, NCJ-83736, 1982.

Electronic Funds Transfer Association (EFTA). "Fed Announces Final Revision to Official Reg E Staff Commentary". Washington Report, 9 May 1985(a).

Electronic Funds Transfer Association (EFTA). "OCC Speaks Out On 'Excessive' ATM Fees." Executive Report, 22 July 1985(b).

Ellis, M.B. and Greguras, F.M. The Electronic Fund Transfer Act and Federal Reserve Board Regulation E: A Compliance Guide for Financial Institutuions. Englewood Cliffs, New Jersey: Prentice-Hall, Inc., 1983.

Federal Deposit Insurance Corporation.   1983 Statistics on Banking. Washington, D.C.: author, 1984.

Federal Reserve Board.   Annual Report, 1983. Washington, D.C.: author, 1984.

Ferris, T.   "Study Finds That the Rising Fear Over EFT Fraud is not Justified by Incidents." American Banker, 3 December 1984.

Ferris, T. "Risk Seen in Automated Clearing." American Banker, 17 April 1985(a).

Ferris, T.   "Fed Warning On West Coast Wire Fraud". American Banker, 22 August 1985(b).

Gallant, J.   "ATM Code Fluke Spurs $40,000 Theft." Computerworld, 8 October 1984.

Garsson, R.M.   "Two Consultants' Totals Vary For Nation's Teller Machines." American Banker, 10 August 1983.

Government Data Systems. "On-Line Contracts, Personnel, Studies." May 1985.

Matthews, G.   "ATM Bomb Blast Damages NY Bank." American Banker, 20 September 1983.

Miller, D.   "Army Looks For Reliability, Simplicity From ATM Handprint Reader." Bank Systems and Equipment, November 1984.

Misra, P.   "Safeguarding EFT Networks". Computers in Banking, September 1984.

Myers, N.   "Point of Confusion." Computers in Banking, September 1984.

Nilson, H.S. The Nilson Report. Los Angeles, CA: No. 347, January 1985.

Parker, D.   and Nycum, S.   Computer Crime: Criminal Justice Resource Manual.   Washington, D.C.: Government Printing Office, 1979.

Parker, D.   "Computer Abuse Research Update." Computer/Law Journal 2(1980).

Perry, T.S.   and Wallich, P. "Can Computer Crime Be Stopped?". IEEE Spectrum, May 1984.

Polmer, H.M. and Epperson, G.M. "ATM Interchange Confronts the Law: Challenges to Authority, Structure and Competition." Electronic Funds Transfer Association. Washington, D.C.: author, 1981.

Shea, T. "Banks Vulnerable to Determined Hackers." Infoworld, 26 March 1984.

Tien, J.M. and Cahn, M.F. "Commerical Security Field Test Program: A Systemic Evaluation of the Impact of Security Surveys", chapter in Major Evaluations in Community Crime Prevention (editor: D.P. Rosenbaum). Beverly Hills, CA: Sage Publications, submitted 1983.

Tien, J.M., Fosque, G.L., Cahn, M.F., and Colton, K.W. Special Report: Electronic Fund Transfer and Crime. Washington, D.C.: Bureau of Justice Statistics, NCJ-92650, February 1984.

Tien, J.M., Rich, T.F., Cahn, M.F., and Kaplan, C.G. Special Report: Electronic Fund Transfer Fraud. Washington, D.C.: Bureau of Justice Statistics, NCJ-96666, March 1985.

Tyson, D.O. "Video Banking Grows Rapidly Since January." American Banker, 4 June 1985.

Weinstein, M. "U.S. Studies Cost of ATM Fraud". American Banker, 11 March 1985(a).

Weinstein, M. "ATM User Safeguards Criticized." American Banker, 10 April 1985(b).

Zimmer, L.F. "ATM Boom Ahead." Magazine of Bank Administration, May 1979.

Zimmer, L.F. "ATM Acceptance Grows." Magazine of Bank Administration, May 1981.

Zimmer, L.F. "1983 ATM Update." Magazine of Bank Administration, May 1983.

Zimmer, L.F. "ATMs 1983: A Critical Assessment." Magazine of Bank Administration, May 1984.

Zimmer, L.F. "ATMs 1984: A Time for Opportunity." Magazine of Bank Administration, May 1985.

A DATA COLLECTION INSTRUMENTS

Five exhibits are contained in this appendix; they consist of the data collection instruments used in this study (i.e., ATM: Incident Data Collection Instrument, ATM: Summary Data Collection Instrument, Wire Transfer: Incident Data Collection Instrument, Wire Transfer: Summary Data Collection Instrument, and Wire Transfer: Attitudinal Data Collection Instrument). Where meaningful, the number of responses, as well as the resultant distribution and average or mean, are displayed in italics.

ATM: Incident Data Collection Instrument

This form is in 5 parts: Parts A (Background) and B (Transaction and Disposition must be completed for every error/claim; Part C (Deposit-Related Information) must be completed if the error/claim involves a disputed deposit; Part D (Withdrawal-Related Information) must be completed if the error/claim involves a disputed withdrawal; and Part E (Regulation E Requirements) must be completed if Regulation E applies. Further, the right-hand side of the form has been set aside for entering the corresponding dates and narrative information.

A. BACKGROUND

1. Case No.:_____   Date Report Taken:___/___/___

2. Accountholder (A/H) Information
   Name:_____ Sex: $N=3596$ M= 51.1%
   Address:_____   F= 48.9

   _____
   Telephone: Home_____ Work_____
   Card Number:_____
   Number of Cards Issued:_____

3. Account(s) Information

Number	Type	Joint Account Name

4. A/H's Bank Contact   Date Contact Made:___/___/___
   Branch Identifier:_____
   Name/Position of Contact:_____
   Telephone:_____

5. Reason for Initiating Error/Claim $N=4185$ Date Initiated:___/___/___
   IF A/H-Initiated:
   Lost/Stolen/Missing Card   0.2%
   Deposit Not Credited   14.4
   Deposit Credited, But Erroneously   2.8
   Shorted/Over on Withdrawal
     (Dispensing)   26.0
   Shorted/Over on Withdrawal
     (Posting)   3.8
   Unauthorized Withdrawal(s)   43.2
   Other_____   0.9

   IF Bank-Initiated:
   Overdraft   6.0
   Empty Envelope Deposited   0.9
   Amount Deposited Different Than
     That Indicated on Envelope and/or
     That Keyed Into ATM   0.1
   Uncollectable Check Deposited   0.5
   Stolen/Fraudulent Check Deposited   1.1
   Other_____   0.1

6. Has A/H Completed An Affidavit (or Equivalent)? Yes _46.6%_ No _53.4_

N=3849

Date Affidavit (or Equivalent) Signed: __/__/__

B. TRANSACTION AND DISPOSITION

7. Transaction History:

TRANS. DATE/TIME	TRANS. TYPE[1]	ATM#/ WHOSE ATM?	AMOUNT A/H STATES: DEPOSITED	WITHDRAWN	AMOUNT POSTED (+/−)	POSTING DATE	BANK DETERM.[2]

[1] Transaction type: D (deposit) or W (withdrawal, including overdrafts)
[2] For each disputed transaction, bank determines if: A (authorized) or U (unauthorized)

8. Disposition Summary

AMOUNT CLAIMED OWED TO:		INITIAL DISPOSITION AMOUNTS A/H		BANK	
A/H	BANK	CRED.	"LOSS"	RECOV.	"LOSS"
2090	419	2127	1717	95	1000
232.4	341.1	241.5	191.4	304.6	356.6
FINAL DISPOSITION AMOUNTS					

N=
Mean=

Date of Initial Disposition: __/__/__

Date of Final Disposition: __/__/__

9. Information Concerning Initial Disposition Amounts   N=1393

a. If A/H's Claim was Partially or Completely Denied, The Reason Was:

A/H Confused or Withdrew Claim	30.1%
A/H Had Card In Possession and Made Transactions	26.3
A/H Had Card In Possession But Did Not Make Transactions	11.4
A/H Revealed PIN to Person	4.3
A/H Claimed PIN was Secure	2.0
A/H Could Not Provide Sufficient Information	3.7
Bank Had No Record of Transaction(s)	8.8
Other_____	13.4

b. Did Regulation E Liability Affect *N=2786*
Disposition Amounts? Yes_11.4_No_88.6_

10. Which Event Occurred Between Initial
and Final Dispositions?
A/H Accepted Initial Disposition   *N=3628*
   (i.e., No Further Action)   97.4%
A/H Appealed to Higher Bank Authority _1.0_
A/H Appealed In Court   _0.0_
A/H and Bank Settled Out-of-Court   _0.0_
Bank Turned Claim Over to Collection
   Agency   _0.1_
Bank Reconsidered After Further
   Investigation   _0.5_
Other_____   _1.0_

11. Other Department(s) In the Bank That This   Date of Referral:__/__/__
Error/Claim Has Been Referred To: *N=511*
   Security/Investigations Office   99.8%
   Other_____   _0.2_

<u>C.   DEPOSIT-RELATED INFORMATION</u>

12. Cause of Deposit-Related Error/Claim *N=734*
A/H Deposited Empty Envelope   _5.8%_
A/H Deposited in Wrong Account   _11.6_
A/H Deposited Amount Different Than
   That Indicated On Envelope and/or
   That Keyed Into ATM   _10.3_
A/H Deposited Uncollectable Check   _4.8_
A/H Deposited Stolen/Fraudulent Check _1.7_
A/H Confused — No Error   _22.9_
Bank Posted Incorrect Amount   _13.5_
Bank Posted to Wrong Account   _4.5_
Person Other Than A/H Made Bad
   Deposit   _15.7_
Other_____   _9.2_

<u>D.   WITHDRAWAL-RELATED INFORMATION</u>

13. Cause of Withdrawal-Related Error/Claim
A/H Had Card Lost/Stolen (Causing   *N=3277*
   Unauthorized Transaction)   _28.9%_
A/H Had Card In Possession But
   Transaction Unauthorized   _14.7_
A/H Withdrew Against Insufficient/
   Bad Deposit (Causing Overdraft)   _2.0_
A/H Confused — No Error   _13.1_
Bank's Computer Was Off-line
   (Causing Overdraft)   _5.6_
Bank's Delayed Posting Procedure
   (Causing Overdraft)   _1.0_
Bank's ATM Had Mechanical Problem
   (Causing Shorted/Over Withdrawal
   or Wrong Posting)   _32.0_
Other_____   _2.7_

14. IF A/H Claims Withdrawal(s) Were
    Unauthorized, Was Card In The Possession
    Of A/H At Time of Withdrawal(s)? *N=1907*
    Yes _47.0_% No _53.0_

    IF "NO", ALSO COMPLETE SECTION D.1 (CARD
    NOT-IN-POSSESSION INFORMATION)

15. IF A/H Claims Withdrawal(s) Were   Date Photographs Ordered: __/__/__
    Unauthorized, Are Photographs of Person
    Making Withdrawal(s) Available?   *N=1657*
    Yes, And Person Has Been Identified _6.6_%
    Yes, But Person Cannot Be Identified _9.4_
    No, Because ATM Does Not Have Photo
       Equipment   _83.7_
    No, Because ATM's Photo Equipment
       Was Out-of-Order   _0.3_

16. IF A/H Claims Withdrawal(s) Were
    Unauthorized, Is Person Making
    Withdrawal(s): *N=1779*
       Unknown _53.5_% Suspected _27.0_ Known _19.5_

17. IF A/H Claims Withdrawal(s) Were
    Unauthorized and Person Making With-
    drawal(s) Is Suspected/Known, How Is
    The Person Related to the A/H? *N=789*
    Same Person   _63.1_% Girl/Boy Friend _5.6_
    Spouse   _2.9_   Child   _7.6_
    Ex-Spouse   _1.3_   No Relationship _6.1_
                          Other_____ _13.4_

D.1   CARD NOT-IN-POSSESSION INFORMATION

18. Card Status At Time of Unauthorized   Date Card Initially
    Withdrawal(s):   *N=1011*   Received:__/__/__
    Lost   _24.4_%   Date Card Actually
    Stolen   _65.7_   Missing: __/__/__
    Never Received   _8.5_   Date Card Discovered
    Other_____   _1.4_   Missing: __/__/__
                                                 Date A/H Notified Bank:
                                                    __/__/__
                                                 Date A/H Notified Police:
                                                    __/__/__

19. PIN Status At Time of Unauthorized   Date PIN Initially
    Withdrawal(s)   Received:__/__/__
    a. PIN Kept: *N=650*
       On Card   _5.2_%
       Near Card (In Wallet/Purse) _64.1_
       Written Down Elsewhere _11.8_
       Not Written Down   _18.9_
    b. PIN Revealed To: *N=451*   Date PIN Revealed:__/__/__
       No One   _69.6_%
       Family Member or Friend _19.9_
       A Person Impersonating A Bank
          Officer   _3.2_
       Other Unknown Person   _4.2_
       Other_____ _3.1_

20. IF Card Was Lost/Stolen, Where Did It
    Occur?   N=590
    Home   26.8% Parking Lot   1.2
    Car   16.4   Retail Place   17.4
    Street   9.7   School   5.2
    Work Place   11.6   Other_____11.2

21. IF Card Was Stolen, The Theft Resulted
    In: N=590
    Only Card Being Stolen   29.0%
    Card and Wallet/Purse Being Stolen   61.4
    Card, Wallet/Purse, and Other
       Things Being Stolen   9.6

22. Upon Receiving Notification, Did Bank   Date "Hot Card" Implemented:
    "Hot Card"? N=596   __/__/__
       Yes 99.7 No 0.3

23. What Is The Current Card Status?   N=162
    A/H Found It   5.6%
    Still Outstanding   59.8
    Hot-Carded and Destroyed   9.3   Date "Hot Card" Captured:
    Hot-Carded and Returned to A/H   13.0   __/__/__
    Card Found and Returned to Bank   9.8
    Other_____   2.5

E. REGULATION E REQUIREMENTS

This section covers two important provisions of Regulation E — error/claim
resolution dates and A/H liability for unauthorized transactions. For further
guidance on these and other related issues, consult the text of Regulation E.

24. Regulation E Error/Claim Resolution
    Dates

    Did A/H Notify Bank of Error/Claim   Date A/H Notified Bank:__/__/__
    Within 60 Calendar Days of Transmittal   Date Statement Transmitted:
    of Periodic Statement Containing Alleged   __/__/__
    Error/Claim?   Date 60 Calendar Days After
                                                     Transmittal:__/__/__
    Yes__ (Error/Claim Must Be Completed
          Within 10 Business Days After A/H
          Notifies Bank   Date 10 Business Days After
               or   Notification (Provisional
          Provisional Credit Must Be Granted   Credit):__/__/__
          Within 10 Business Days After A/H   Date 45 Calendar Days After
          Notifies Bank and Error/Claim   Notification (Resolution:)__/__/__
          Resolution Must Be Completed With-
          in 45 Calendar Days After A/H
          Notifies Bank)
    No__ (Regulation E Error/Claim Solution
          Dates Do Not Apply)

94

25. A/H Liability for Unauthorized Transactions

    a. Did A/H Notify Bank of Missing Card Within 2 Business Days After Discovering it Missing?

    Yes _____   No _____

    b. Did A/H Notify Bank of Alleged Error/ Claim Within 60 Calendar Days of Transmittal of Periodic Statement Containing Unauthorized Transactions?

    Yes _____   No _____

Answer to Question		Maximum A/H Liability
25a	25b	
Yes	Yes	$ 50
No	Yes	$500
Yes	No	$ 50 + $X
No	No	$500 + $X

$X = Amount of Unauthorized Transactions Occurring After 60th Calendar Day After Transmittal of Periodic Statement Containing Unauthorized Transactions

Date Card Discovered Missing: __/__/__

Date Bank Notified: __/__/__

Dates: Same As Those Corresponding to Question 24

Exhibit A.2

ATM: Summary Data Collection Instrument

Panel Bank No.:_____

			1983	1984
1.	Number of Installed ATMs (End of Year)		_____	_____
2.	a)	Number of Transactions (On Bank's ATMS)		
		Withdrawals	_____	_____
		Deposits	_____	_____
		Total	_____	_____
	b)	Dollar Volume of Transactions (On Bank's ATMS)		
		Withdrawals	_____	_____
		Deposits	_____	_____
		Total	_____	_____
3.	a)	Number of Incidents Resulting in Dollar Loss to Bank		
		Fraud-Related	_____	_____
		Non-Fraud-Related	_____	_____
		Total	_____	_____
	b)	Dollar Amount of Loss to Bank		
		Fraud-Related	_____	_____
		Non-Fraud-Related	_____	_____
		Total	_____	_____
	c)	Dollar Amount of Recovery	_____	_____

Exhibit A.3

Wire Transfer: Incident Data Collection Instrument

For PSB Use Only:
Bank Code: [ ][ ][ ]   Case No.: [ ][ ][ ]

A. INCIDENT CHARACTERISTICS

1. Please Check the Most Appropriate Description of the Incident: *N=207*

2.9% [ ] Successful Fraudulent Transfer (Entry, Alteration or Destruction)

3.4 [ ] Attempted Fraudulent Transfer

52.2 [ ] Inadvertent Error Leading to Fraudulent Absconding with Funds

41.5 [ ] Inadvertent Error Leading to Exposure Without Loss of Principal

2. Type of Incident: *N=182*

8.2% [ ] External Error in Message Initiation

37.5 [ ] Bank Error in Message Delivery

13.2 [ ] Bank Error in Message Content

2.7 [ ] Bank Error in Message Interpretation

14.8 [ ] Bank Error in Customer Notification

9.9 [ ] Bank Error in Accounting Entries

5.5 [ ] Failure to Follow Established Procedures

1.1 [ ] Transaction Fraudulently Entered (Internally)

4.4 [ ] Transaction Fraudulently Entered (Externally)

0.5 [ ] Transaction Altered in Processing

0.0 [ ] Fraudulent Destruction of Transaction Records

2.2 [ ] Other____________________ (specify)

3. Date of First Occurrence: [ ][ ]/[ ][ ]/[ ][ ]
(mm) (dd) (yy)

4. Date of Discovery: [ ][ ]/[ ][ ]/[ ][ ]
(mm) (dd) (yy)

5. Discovered By: *N=181*

33.1% [ ] Central Wire Transfer Operation

1.7 [ ] Branch Bank

11.6 [ ] Other Bank

31.5 [ ] Sender

13.3 [ ] Receiver

8.8 [ ] Other____________________ (specify)

B. TRANSACTION DATA

1. Transaction Initiated By: $N=180$

28.9% [ ] Telephone   3.3 [ ] Customer Terminal Link

3.3 [ ] Walk-In   0.0 [ ] Customer CPU Link

3.3 [ ] Mail   32.3 [ ] Funds Transfer Network

1.7 [ ] Messenger   23.3 [ ] Telex

0.0 [ ] Facsimile Equipment   0.0 [ ] TWX

0.0 [ ] Internal Bank Computer   3.9 [ ] Other_____
                                                    (specify)

2. Transaction was: $N=182$

61.0% [ ] Domestic   39.0 [ ] International

3. Type of Transaction: $N=182$

33.0% [ ] Inbound 63.2 [ ] Outbound   2.7 [ ] Intrabank   1.1 [ ] Advice

4. Primary Network Involved in Incident: $N=148$

66.9% [ ] Fedwire 12.2 [ ] Bankwire 5.4 [ ] CHIPS 10.8 [ ] SWIFT 4.7 [ ] Telex

5. Nature of Transaction: $N=180$

45.6% [ ] Customer Transfer   2.8 [ ] Reverse Money Transfer

13.9 [ ] Bank-to-Bank Transfer   0.5 [ ] Reversal

22.2 [ ] Bank Transfer in Favor   7.8 [ ] Other_____
     of 3rd Bank   (specify)

7.2 [ ] Advice to Credit

6. Processing Locations:

             From-   To-

Country_____   _____

City_____   _____

State_____   _____

C. REASON FOR INCIDENT

1. Incident Cause: *N=206*

0.0% [ ] Call-Back Failure		37.3 [ ] Message Duplicated	
0.5 [ ] Collusion (Internal)		17.5 [ ] Message Misrouted	
2.4 [ ] Collusion (External)		0.5 [ ] Misuse of ID or Pasword	
0.5 [ ] Data Line Compromise		0.0 [ ] Payment Made Without Proper ID	
0.0 [ ] Transfer Dollar Limits Exceeded		0.0 [ ] PIN or Token Compromised	
1.0 [ ] Signature Forged		0.0 [ ] Scissored Telex	
9.2 [ ] Entry Passed to Wrong Account		0.0 [ ] Test Key Compromised	
4.9 [ ] Incorrect Currency		1.0 [ ] Test Word Not Validated	
9.7 [ ] Incorrect Amount		0.0 [ ] Unauthorized Access to Operations Area	
2.9 [ ] Insufficient Funds		0.0 [ ] Unauthorized Alteration of Database	
3.9 [ ] Message Altered		0.5 [ ] Uncollected Funds	
		8.2 [ ] Other_____ (specify)	

2. Incident Caused By: *N=201*

90.5% [ ] Bank Employee(s)	0.0 [ ] Software Vendor
3.0 [ ] Corporate Customer	1.5 [ ] Funds Transfer Network
2.0 [ ] Individual Customer	1.0 [ ] Bank Computer System
0.0 [ ] Programmer	2.0 [ ] Other_____ (specify)
0.0 [ ] Hardware Vendor	

D. EXPOSURE/LOSS INFORMATION

1. Amount of Exposure (i.e., Potential Loss) to Bank: *N=175*

$ [ ][ ],[ ][ ][ ],[ ][ ][ ] *Average= $942,450*
(amount in U.S. dollars)

2. Did Incident Result in Loss of Principal to Bank? *N=182*

48.9% [ ] No   51.1 [ ] Yes - $ [ ][ ],[ ][ ][ ],[ ][ ][ ] *Average= $29,718*
(amount in U.S. dollars)

3. Has There Been Any Recovery of the Lost Principal? *N=92*

66.3% [ ] No   33.7 [ ] Yes - $ [ ][ ],[ ][ ][ ],[ ][ ][ ] *Average= $46,907*
(amount in U.S. dollars)

E. BANK ACTION

1. Were Procedural or Systems Changes Instituted as a Result of the Incident?:
N=176

83.8% [ ] No   10.2[ ] Yes (please describe in F.)

2. Has Any Wire Transfer Employee Resigned or Been Terminated or Transferred as a Result of the Incident?: N=175

99.4% [ ] No   0.6[ ] Yes (please describe in F.)

3. Has any non-Wire Transfer Employee Resigned or Been Terminated as a Result of the Incident?: N=173

98.8% [ ] No   1.2[ ] Yes (please describe in F.)

4. Has Any Change in Wire Transfer Management Personnel Been Instituted as a Result of the Incident?: N=175

100.0% [ ] No   0.0[ ] Yes (please describe in F.)

5. Has the Bank Instituted Any Civil Legal Action as a Result of the Incident?:
N=179

86.6% [ ] No   13.4[ ] Yes (please describe in F.)

6. Has Any Prosecution Resulted from Criminal Legal Action Taken as a Result of the Incident?: N=173

97.7% [ ] No   2.3[ ] Yes (please describe in F.)

F. GENERAL COMMENTS

Please provide additional incident-related information not reflected in the previous sections. Use reverse side if necessary.

_____

_____

_____

_____

_____

_____

_____

_____

Exhibit A.4

Wire Transfer: Summary Data Collection Instrument

Panel Bank No.:_____ (For each entry, please indicate "domestic/international")

	1983	1984
1. a) Number of Wire Transfers		
In	_____/_____	_____/_____
Out	_____/_____	_____/_____
Total	_____/_____	_____/_____
b) Dollar Amount of Wire Transfers		
In	_____/_____	_____/_____
Out	_____/_____	_____/_____
Total	_____/_____	_____/_____
2. a) Number of Exposure Incidents (Leading to Either Loss or No Loss)		
In	_____/_____	_____/_____
Out	_____/_____	_____/_____
Total	_____/_____	_____/_____
b) Dollar Amount of Exposure (For Both Loss and No Loss Incidents)		
In	_____/_____	_____/_____
Out	_____/_____	_____/_____
Total	_____/_____	_____/_____
3. a) Number of Loss Incidents		
In	_____/_____	_____/_____
Out	_____/_____	_____/_____
Total	_____/_____	_____/_____
b) Dollar Amount of Loss (Principal)		
In	_____/_____	_____/_____
Out	_____/_____	_____/_____
Total	_____/_____	_____/_____
c) Dollar Amount of Loss (Compensation)		
In	_____/_____	_____/_____
Out	_____/_____	_____/_____
Total	_____/_____	_____/_____
d) Dollar Amount of Recovery		
Total	_____/_____	_____/_____

Exhibit A.5

Wire Transfer: Attitudinal Data Collection Instrument

 Public Systems Evaluation, Inc.

SURVEY INSTRUMENT: FRAUD AND LOSS IN WIRE TRANSFER

PREPARED FOR ATTENDEES AT BANK ADMINISTRATION INSTITUTE'S

MONEY TRANSFER DEVELOPMENTS CONFERENCE '83

Those of you who are associated with a bank are cordially invited to contribute to an on-going study -- on the nature and extent of fraud and loss in electronic funds transfer (EFT) -- by completing this survey instrument. (Please coordinate and complete only one instrument per bank.) The study -- being conducted by Public Systems Evaluation, Inc. (PSE) and with the participation of the Association of Reserve City Bankers (ARCB) and a panel of 18 of its large member banks -- involves the collection and analysis of detailed incident-based data in both the EFT retail (i.e., automated teller machine, point-of-sale, telephone bill paying, and home banking) and EFT corporate (i.e., wire transfer, automated clearing house, and cash management) areas. Your responses will supplement our panel findings in the wire transfer area.

Please take a few minutes now to complete this brief, 8-question survey instrument. After completion, please send the instrument to PSE in the envelope provided. Should you require it, our address is Public Systems Evaluation, Inc., 929 Massachusetts Avenue, Cambridge, Massachusetts 02139, (617) 547-7620. Remember that your individual responses will remain completely confidential -- only a summary of all responses to each question will be reported.

Finally, we would like to thank each of you in advance for your cooperation and participation in this important study.

N = 73 unless other sample size is indicated

---

1. To what extent is your bank's wire transfer operation automated?

	Fully Automated (Computer Link)	Partially Automated (Terminal Link)	Not Automated (Telephone Link)	No Data
•Currently, my bank's wire operation is:	46.7%	47.9	2.7	2.7
•In 5 years, I expect my bank's wire operation to be:	74.0%	12.3	0.0	13.7

2. What do you estimate the size of your bank's wire transfer (domestic and international) operation to be?

    •Currently, I estimate the average <u>daily number</u> of transfers (in + out + book) to be 2,195.

    •Currently, I estimate the average <u>daily dollar</u> volume of transfers (in + out + book) to be $ 6.2 B .

3. What is the <u>annual</u> amount of wire transfer related fraud and loss in your bank?

    •Currently, I estimate the annual amount to be $ 8,327 .

    •In 5 years and <u>assuming</u> the current level of automation in my bank's wire transfer operation, I estimate the annual amount to be $ 19,003 .

4. To what extent do you think each of the following causes of wire transfer fraud and loss has <u>contributed</u> to the annual amount of fraud and loss?

Cause	In terms of the current fraud and loss levels, I feel that the stated cause contributed:						In 5 years and assuming the current level of automation in my bank's wire transfer operation, I would expect the stated cause to contribute:					
	Very significantly	Significantly	Moderately	Slightly	Not At All	Don't Know	Very significantly	Significantly	Moderately	Slightly	Not At All	Don't Know
Call-Back Failure	12.3%	11.0	2.7	12.3	35.6	26.0	5.5%	16.4	11.0	15.1	20.5	31.5
Collusion (Internal)	4.1%	4.1	2.7	6.8	50.7	31.5	1.4%	6.8	13.7	9.6	23.3	45.2
Collusion (External)	6.8%	8.2	6.8	5.5	38.4	34.2	4.1%	11.0	11.0	6.8	20.5	46.6
Data Line Compromise	0.0%	0.0	6.8	6.8	56.2	30.1	8.2%	4.1	11.0	5.5	30.1	41.1
Transfer Dollar Limits Exceeded	1.4%	2.7	4.1	11.0	53.4	27.4	2.7%	4.1	11.0	15.1	37.1	30.1
Signature Forged	4.1%	2.7	1.4	11.0	53.4	27.4	2.7%	1.4	0.0	19.2	34.2	42.5
Entry Passed to Wrong Account	11.0%	8.2	23.3	20.5	13.7	23.3	2.7%	8.2	19.2	31.5	9.6	28.8
Insufficient Funds	1.4%	5.5	5.5	24.7	35.6	27.4	0.0%	6.8	15.1	17.8	28.8	31.5
Message Altered	1.4%	0.0	9.6	5.5	56.2	27.4	4.1%	6.8	5.5	12.3	35.6	35.6
Message Duplicated	12.3%	6.8	13.7	21.9	21.9	23.3	5.5%	2.7	17.8	21.9	17.8	34.2
Message Misrouted	4.1%	12.3	16.4	26.0	17.8	23.3	6.8%	6.8	21.9	19.2	15.1	30.1
Misuse of I.D. or Password	1.4%	2.7	8.2	11.0	50.7	26.0	1.4%	1.4	9.6	15.1	37.0	35.6
Payment Made Without Proper I.D.	2.7%	2.7	6.8	12.3	46.6	28.8	2.7%	2.7	6.8	19.2	28.8	39.7
PIN or Token Compromised	1.4%	2.7	4.1	5.5	52.1	34.2	2.7%	6.8	1.4	12.3	31.5	45.2
Scissored Telex	0.0%	0.0	4.1	6.8	50.7	38.4	1.4%	0.0	1.4	13.7	38.4	45.2
Test Key Compromised	1.4%	1.4	2.7	5.5	56.2	32.9	1.4%	2.7	4.1	16.4	37.0	38.4
Test Word Not Validated	0.0%	2.7	1.4	13.7	52.1	30.1	1.4%	0.0	6.8	19.2	32.9	39.7
Unauthorized Access to Operations Area	1.4%	1.4	1.4	8.2	61.6	26.0	2.7%	0.0	2.7	15.1	47.9	31.5
Unauthorized Alteration of Data Base	1.4%	1.4	1.4	8.2	57.5	30.1	2.7%	1.4	9.6	11.0	30.1	45.2
Uncollected Funds	2.7%	4.1	4.1	19.2	42.5	27.4	4.1%	5.5	12.3	12.3	28.8	37.0
Other (_____ Specify)	—	—	—	—	—	—	—	—	—	—	—	—
Other (_____ Specify)	—	—	—	—	—	—	—	—	—	—	—	—

103

5. To what extent do you feel each of the following procedures has prevented incidents of wire transfer fraud and loss?

Procedure	In terms of the current types of fraud and loss incidents, I feel that the stated procedure has prevented such incidents:							If implemented appropriately, I feel that the stated procedure could prevent such incidents:					
	Very Significantly	Significantly	Moderately	Slightly	Not At All	Don't Know	Not Implemented	Very Significantly	Significantly	Moderately	Slightly	Not At All	Don't Know
Call-Back Verification of Transfer Requests	37.0%	20.5	17.8	8.2	5.5	1.4	9.6	30.1%	19.2	11.0	2.7	1.4	35.6
Use of Test Keys/PINs When Customer Originates by Phone	28.8%	27.4	13.7	4.1	4.1	4.1	17.8	30.1%	12.3	6.8	8.2	2.7	39.7
Use of Test Keys/PINs Between Banks	23.3%	28.8	16.4	13.7	8.2	2.7	6.8	23.3%	15.1	12.3	8.2	2.7	38.4
Use of Test Keys/PINs in Phone Notification	17.8%	16.4	11.0	11.0	12.3	5.5	26.0	19.2%	16.4	12.3	8.2	4.1	39.7
Establishing Customer Specific Transfer Restrictions	23.3%	19.2	30.1	8.2	2.7	5.5	11.0	23.3%	16.4	17.8	1.4	1.4	39.7
Increased Use of Pre-Formatted, Repetitive Transfers	24.7%	32.9	19.2	9.6	5.5	1.4	6.8	26.0%	20.5	5.5	5.5	4.1	38.4
Restrictions on Account Officer Transfer Initiation	15.1%	15.1	20.5	16.4	6.8	6.8	19.2	17.8%	15.1	15.1	8.2	4.1	39.7
Keystroke Verification	15.1%	8.2	8.2	9.6	11.0	15.1	32.9	15.1%	9.6	9.6	6.8	8.2	50.7
Tape Recording of Phone Activity	20.5%	37.0	24.7	8.2	5.5	1.4	2.7	19.2%	15.1	15.1	8.2	4.1	38.4
Physically Securing Operational Area	30.1%	19.2	23.3	16.4	5.5	2.7	2.7	26.0%	12.3	12.3	6.8	2.7	39.7
Physical Control of Operational Area	21.9%	31.5	19.2	21.9	0.0	2.7	2.7	17.8%	19.2	12.3	8.2	1.4	41.1
Software Control and Logging of Terminal Access/Transactions	26.0%	34.2	9.6	6.8	4.1	5.5	13.7	19.2%	31.5	2.7	4.1	0.0	42.5
Separation of Personnel Duties	27.4%	26.0	27.4	11.0	1.4	2.7	4.1	26.0%	19.2	12.3	1.4	0.0	41.1
Careful Background Screening of New Personnel	16.4%	26.0	24.7	24.7	2.7	1.4	4.1	19.2%	17.8	19.2	5.5	0.0	38.4
External/Internal Data Line Encryption	2.7%	5.5	9.6	15.1	11.0	12.3	43.8	23.3%	16.4	12.3	5.5	5.5	37.0
Quality Control and Audit of Software	5.5%	16.4	21.9	11.0	8.2	19.2	17.8	15.1%	21.9	12.3	4.1	1.4	45.2
Improved Supervision of Wire Transfer Operations	32.9%	46.6	13.7	4.1	1.4	1.4	0.0	38.4%	15.1	6.8	1.4	0.0	38.4
Well Defined and Enforced Internal Procedures	42.5%	41.1	11.0	4.1	0.0	1.4	0.0	39.7%	17.8	4.1	0.0	0.0	38.4
Other (_____) Specify													
Other (_____) Specify													

6. What is your current position at the bank? My current position is:

   __0.0%__ Funds Transfer Planner

   __78.1__ Funds Transfer Manager

   __1.4__ Funds Transfer System Designer

   __0.0__ Funds Transfer Security Specialist

   __4.1__ Bank Auditor

   __13.7__ Other (_____)

                                    Specify

   __2.7__ No Data

7. Would you be willing to have PSE contact you about providing detailed incident-specific wire transfer fraud and loss data to assist the study?

   __45.2%__ No

   __47.9__ Yes, you may contact me at:

   __6.9__ No Data

   Name _____

   Title _____

   Address _____

   City _____ State _____ Zip _____

   Telephone (_____) _____

8. Do you have any other comments to make about wire transfer fraud and loss?

   _____

   _____

   _____

   _____

   _____